DATE DUE

POWER YOUR HAPPY

POWER YOUR HAPPY

Work Hard, Play Nice, and Build Your
Dream Life

LISA SUGAR

DUTTON

DUTTON

An imprint of Penguin Random House LLC
375 Hudson Street
New York, New York 10014

Copyright © 2016 by Lisa Sugar

LIBRARY OF CONGRESS CATALOGING-IN-PUBLICATION DATA

Names: Sugar, Lisa, author.
Title: Power your happy : work hard, play nice, and build your dream life /
    Lisa Sugar.
Description: 1st [edition]. | New York : Dutton, a member of Penguin
    Random House LLC, 2016.
Identifiers: LCCN 2016020264 (print) | LCCN 2016024857 (ebook) |
    ISBN 9781101985069 (hardcover) | ISBN 9781101985076 (epub) |
    ISBN 9781101986080 (Target ed.)
Subjects: LCSH: Happiness. | Self-realization. | Success.
Classification: LCC BF575.H27 S84 2016 (print) | LCC BF575.H27
    (ebook) | DDC 158—dc23
LC record available at https://lccn.loc.gov/2016020264

Printed in the United States of America
10 9 8 7 6 5 4 3 2 1

Set in Linotype Syntax Serif Com
Designed by Cassandra Garruzzo
Illustrations by Sara Combs

*To the love of my life, my partner and best friend, Brian,
who has helped create the ultimate dream life, including my
three favorite people—our daughters Katie, Juliet, and
Elle—who taught me there is no greater love than
the ones you create.*

CONTENTS

TIMELINE

MY LIFE & POP CULTURE INFLUENCES

the early years ...

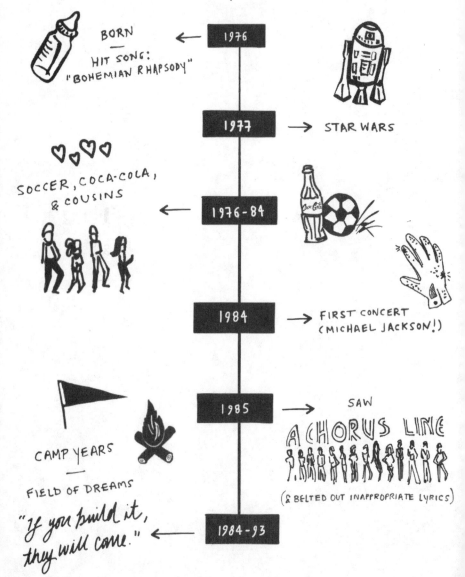

BORN
—
HIT SONG:
"BOHEMIAN RHAPSODY"

1976

→ STAR WARS

1977

SOCCER, COCA-COLA, & COUSINS

1976-84

1984 → FIRST CONCERT (MICHAEL JACKSON!)

1985 → SAW
A CHORUS LINE
(& BELTED OUT INAPPROPRIATE LYRICS)

CAMP YEARS
—
FIELD OF DREAMS

"If you build it, they will come."

1984-93

school days

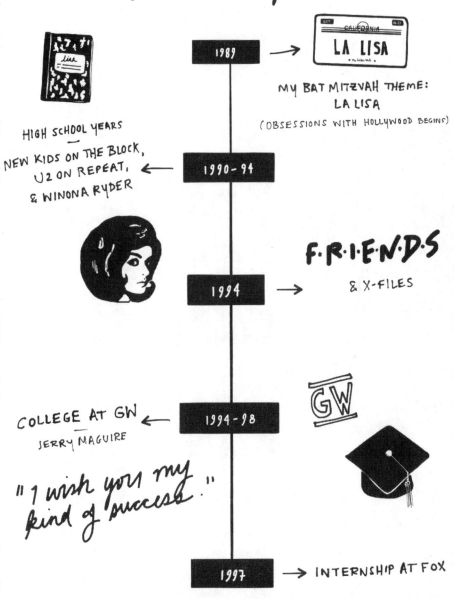

1989 → MY BAT MITZVAH THEME:
LA LISA
(OBSESSIONS WITH HOLLYWOOD BEGINS)

HIGH SCHOOL YEARS
—
NEW KIDS ON THE BLOCK,
U2 ON REPEAT,
& WINONA RYDER
← 1990-94

1994 → F·R·I·E·N·D·S
& X-FILES

COLLEGE AT GW ← 1994-98
JERRY MAGUIRE

"I wish you my
kind of success."

1997 → INTERNSHIP AT FOX

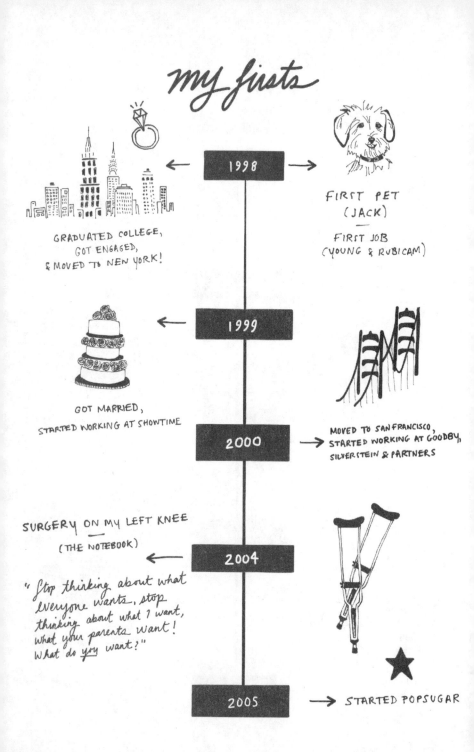

my firsts

1998

GRADUATED COLLEGE,
GOT ENGAGED,
& MOVED TO NEW YORK!

FIRST PET
(JACK)
—
FIRST JOB
(YOUNG & RUBICAM)

1999

GOT MARRIED,
STARTED WORKING AT SHOWTIME

2000

MOVED TO SAN FRANCISCO,
STARTED WORKING AT GOODBY,
SILVERSTEIN & PARTNERS

SURGERY ON MY LEFT KNEE
—
(THE NOTEBOOK)

2004

"Stop thinking about what
everyone wants, stop
thinking about what I want,
what your parents want!
What do you want?"

2005

STARTED POPSUGAR

my "babies"

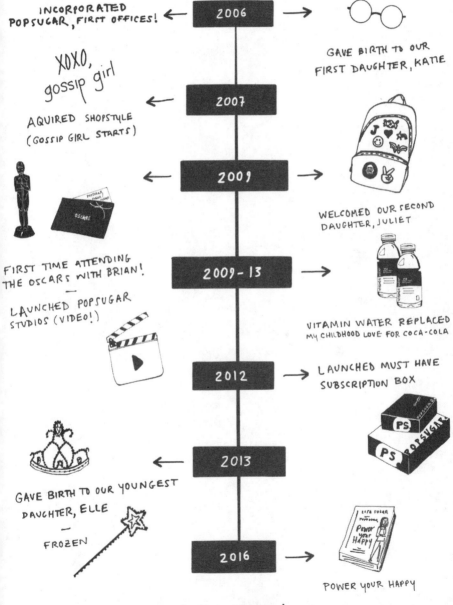

INCORPORATED POPSUGAR, FIRST OFFICES! ← **2006** →

GAVE BIRTH TO OUR FIRST DAUGHTER, KATIE

XOXO, gossip girl

← **2007**

AQUIRED SHOPSTYLE (GOSSIP GIRL STARTS)

← **2009** →

WELCOMED OUR SECOND DAUGHTER, JULIET

FIRST TIME ATTENDING THE OSCARS WITH BRIAN!
—
LAUNCHED POPSUGAR STUDIOS (VIDEO!)

2009-13 →

VITAMIN WATER REPLACED MY CHILDHOOD LOVE FOR COCA-COLA

2012 → LAUNCHED MUST HAVE SUBSCRIPTION BOX

← **2013**

GAVE BIRTH TO OUR YOUNGEST DAUGHTER, ELLE
—
FROZEN

2016 →

POWER YOUR HAPPY

to be continued...

POWER YOUR HAPPY

INTRODUCTION

I know this will be an unpopular opinion, but I can't get behind the phrase "happy Friday." Every week we are bombarded with e-mails and social media updates along the lines of "Fri-YAY!" or "It's Friday, bitches!" or "TGIF!" I love every day; I look forward to Mondays as much as Fridays. In my world, there is no such thing as the Monday blues.

That's not to say I don't appreciate the downtime of weekends, watching my kids' soccer games, overnight getaways, and class with my favorite SoulCycle instructors. Maybe you love weekends for the long brunches or binge-watching TV shows. Those two days do mark a great break in the week, but I also love what I do on the other five days. My ultimate goal has always been to love my family, my "work," and therefore my life.

I also tend not to dwell on how great things were in the

past. While I reflect on the past with warmth, I also look forward to starting the adventure of every day. When I look back at my high school yearbooks, I'm reminded how often I was told that "these will be the best years of your life!" Which made sense at the time: I had no real worries, I was fortunate to be getting a solid education, I had loving parents who put a roof over my head and food on the table. But then I went to college, and life was so much more an adventure; being on my own and away from home felt like the beginning of better years ahead. Then again, when I got married, everyone told me "the best years are ahead!" When I had my first kid, I heard a lot of "cherish this time! These are the best years."

Three daughters, sixteen years of marriage, and one successful media company later, I hope the best years are still to come. Don't get me wrong: the first thirty-nine years of my life have been very fulfilling. But I am only thirty-nine, and there is still a lot on my to-do list. I hope I'm lucky enough to live into my golden years because I hear those are pretty awesome, too.

I want this book to be more about you than me, and I can't tell you what to do next with your life or what your version of success is. But I can share the values I've used to govern my decisions, which I believe have made me a happier and more successful person: working hard and playing nice, being honest and staying positive, taking risks and always evolving, and staying healthy while still indulging in dessert and guilty pleasures, like my fanatical devotion to pop culture. The starting point for everything is something my dad told me all the time: Do what you love.

I know we live in challenging times, and doing what you love is easier said than done. People coming out of college or looking to make a career change have more options than we could have imagined twenty years ago; it's bewildering. But creating your dream life is never easy, and you can't count on luck. Even when you have moments of serendipity, luck is worthless without hard work. Finding your perfect combination of happiness and success won't happen overnight.

I'm not saying I have all the answers, nor is my life the only formula for a great life. But in the ten years since I started POPSUGAR, I've learned a lot about how to build a successful company, hire and mentor talented employees, nurture a happy marriage, and raise children. In sharing what I've learned, I want to help you find what makes you feel happy and fulfilled, to own every day and create a life and a career that you love.

I personally didn't have a career I loved until I was twenty-nine, when I started POPSUGAR. I get asked a lot, "How can I get a cool job like that?" Finding your passion takes time and a shitload of hard work, patience, knowledge, and experience. I didn't know what I wanted "to be when I grew up" until I was twenty-nine.

I can't remember a time when my parents were asking me what I wanted to do with my life. Mostly, they just stressed the importance of continued education. Growing up in Potomac, Maryland, my older brother and I knew that where we went to college was a big thing, and our parents also talked about what I was going to do for grad school, as if that was the only next viable option. My brother is brilliant—math and science genius—but I was a slower learner who struggled in school. What came most naturally to me was always writing, but I never thought that was a viable career. Being tested for learning disabilities in my teens actually got me excited about learning about how people learned. I felt passionate about it, and I decided psychology was my calling.

In 1994, I graduated from high school and went off to study psychology and English at George Washington University in DC. Though "going away to college" didn't take me very far from the DC suburbs where I'd grown up, it was the first step toward creating the life I love—and also a life I never could have expected.

I met my husband, Brian Sugar, when I was a freshman at GW. It was definitely not my intention to meet the man I was going to spend the rest of my life within my first week of college. But I did, and I'm thankful for a million reasons. My college roommate went to high school with Brian, and he wanted to meet her friends and see if any were cute. At the time, I wasn't single, so I was cocky and not interested in potential suitors, and I played it super cool. I won him over playing FIFA soccer on Sega Genesis and actually beating him. Over the next few weeks, and then months, it became obvious to us both that we were meant to be.

Brian has this magnetic personality. He commands a room with a fun, entertaining confidence that you just can't help but listen to. I also admired that he worked hard: He always had a job and loves to talk about how his paper route at the age of twelve helped him invest in baseball cards and comic books, which he sold to buy his first car. Those qualities that first attracted me to him—his work ethic and his people skills—serve us both well today as we run our company, POPSUGAR.

That said, Brian is also a college dropout. After three years at GW, he left to start his first company, an Internet service provider. I was a sophomore at the time, and I had to break the news to my dad, which was not an easy conversation. My dad firmly believed (and still does) that a college education is just the start of figuring out what you want to do in life. But Brian thought differently. He just likes "doing." In fact, he jokes that when he was young, he was always asking his parents and friends, "Doin'?"—his shorthand for "What are you doing?"

Although I didn't follow in Brian's college-dropout footsteps, he did teach me the importance of doing. The ability to "just do it" comes in handy no matter what your life's path, because while you may think you know exactly what you want out of life, you never stop figuring it out.

For instance, I always knew I wanted to be a mom and

have a career, but how my life turned out would have been impossible to predict. As I mentioned before, I never expected to meet the man I would marry at age seventeen. I didn't imagine I would run my own company. I certainly could not have predicted that I would start a company with the man I married! Mostly, I just wanted a life that would make me happy, but the specifics of what a happy life means to me have evolved over the past eighteen years, and I don't expect myself to stop evolving anytime soon, if ever.

When I graduated in 1998, a happy life meant joining Brian in New York and finding a job in the entertainment industry. I'd spent the previous summer interning on *FOX After Breakfast*, a daily morning talk show hosted by Tom Bergeron, and came away convinced that the fast-paced world of entertainment was my calling. I set aside (temporarily, I told myself) my plans for going to grad school for psychology and set my sights on working at a talent agency. But after a few interviews, I realized the culture wasn't for me. The bosses in the corner offices with closed doors reminded me of the law firm where my dad worked; while I loved how passionate he was about his job, I knew that lifestyle wasn't for me and I had to find my own passion.

I expanded my search to marketing firms and advertising agencies and eventually got hired as a media planner at Young & Rubicam. While it wasn't the job in entertainment I had hoped for, it was close enough: My clients included

Sony and Showtime networks, and I was surrounded by creative, smart people who shared my values.

My twenties were defined by jobs I liked but didn't love, but every imperfect experience helped me refine my vision of what I really wanted to do with my life. The most important part of any job is figuring out what you like about it, whether it's the people, the location, the hours, or what you are creating. When I worked in advertising, I loved the creative surroundings and laid-back atmosphere, getting every magazine for free, and seeing new TV shows before anyone else. I looked forward to the days when I got to meet with reps from networks and brands to learn their missions, values, and position in the marketplace. Getting excited about those aspects of the job outweighed the stress of managing budgets, paying invoices, and updating Excel charts all day long.

Even as I was working in advertising, my vague goal of working in entertainment began to come into better focus, so I took the next logical step. After a year at Y&R, I took a similar job at Showtime, and even though my day-to-day duties weren't all that different, it was closer to what I really wanted to do: create content. I wanted to combine my early love of writing with my obsession with pop culture. I decided my dream job was working in the development department of a TV network.

Shortly after I started working at Showtime, I married

Brian. I couldn't wait to embark on the next phase of our life together. By the end of 1999, he got an incredible job offer in San Francisco and we moved across the country, which presented a serious obstacle on my path to working in television. I considered trying to break into magazines, but nothing in San Francisco seemed quite right (and the few places that did weren't interested in hiring me, especially with no experience in the publishing industry yet). So I returned to advertising and spent the next six years working as a media planner at Goodby, Silverstein & Partners. I started to fall in love with the West Coast, raising two Jack Russell terriers while also making human friends. But I couldn't shake the feeling that I wanted to create content and feed my lifelong passion for entertainment.

By 2005, the media world was changing dramatically: Magazines were struggling to figure out online content while new, scrappy websites were launching left and right. For the first time, creating editorial content didn't require getting a job at a magazine or newspaper; you could just start doing it. But no one had created a website that was quite like what I wanted. So I started POPSUGAR, quietly and on the side, while I still had my job at Goodby. At first, I just wanted to see if I could do it and get in the habit of writing every day, but I quickly became addicted to it, and so did my readers.

In November 2005, I found out I was pregnant, and I decided quit my job to devote myself fully to POPSUGAR. In April 2006, Brian and I decided to go all in and turn the website into a business, and a mere two months later, our first daughter, Katie, was born.

It's been an incredible whirlwind since then. Today, POP-SUGAR is a global media empire with five hundred employees, including a variety of businesses: ShopStyle, a shopping destination; Must Have, a monthly subscription box; and POPSUGAR Studios, which produces video content for the web and for TV. POPSUGAR turns ten in 2016, and so does Katie, and as our business has expanded, so has our family: In September 2009, we welcomed our second daughter, Juliet, and in May 2013, I gave birth to our youngest, Elle.

Whether or not your vision of an ideal life involves having a family, figuring out how to balance everything—work, family, romantic relationships, and staying healthy—is a never-ending puzzle. And that's just one piece: You also need to figure out how to balance your passions with your talents, your happiness with success, and having a plan but also not being afraid to change it. I don't really believe in having a five-year-plan—more like an ever-evolving plan that continues to take shape every day. I start every morning with the solid foundation I've built and a vision of the path I need to travel that day.

CHAPTER 1

FIND YOUR PASSION

The phrase *find your passion* is so overused these days, I almost hate to use it here. But when it comes to deciding what you want to do with your life, it's just so damn obvious: You have to find what it is that makes you happy and energized, and it has to be something you want to do every day for hours upon hours. And you might figure that out at the most unexpected moments.

When people find out I'm the founder of POPSUGAR, I often get asked, "How did you do it?" or "How can I get a cool job like that?" Finding your passion takes time—sometimes a decade or two—and your dream job might not even exist yet. Though I found success at a relatively young age, I could never have done at age twenty-two what I did at twenty-nine. But I want you to be able to find it. I want to help you find your perfect intersection of passion and talent.

I'm not saying I have all the answers. In fact, twenty years ago—even ten years ago—I pretty much had zero answers. People came to me for life advice; I was a good listener, so friends would share their relationship issues or vent about work, and I would do my best to take it all in and come up with sound advice. Based on my long-lasting friendships, I'd say I didn't steer anyone majorly in the wrong direction. But what did I really know then? Of course at the time, I thought I knew a lot, but in reality, I was never the smartest kid in school or the biggest overachiever. I was a slower learner with low reading comprehension and was even tested for learning disabilities. I definitely wasn't a straight-A student, and I didn't go to an Ivy League college. But I worked really hard, at least hard enough to get into George Washington University, which I am still very proud of as a life accomplishment. Yet I didn't know what I wanted "to be when I grew up" until—well, until I was twenty-nine.

And I'm here to tell you, it's absolutely OK if you don't know yet either.

In high school and college, I was a total night owl—but not because I was pulling all-nighters to study or staying out all night partying. I much preferred sacrificing sleep to watch late-night talk shows or see a double feature. Back then, I felt like I wasn't good at anything except knowing lots of useless information, like who was going to be in what new TV show or which designer worked at which fashion house. I was the friend everyone turned to when they wanted to know what a celebrity was wearing or doing. People would ask me for advice on beauty products, because I always had something new in my purse. And, of course, I killed it in that game Celebrity—everyone wanted me on their team.

But trusted product recommender and professional celebrity-trivia-game player aren't really viable career options, right?

Turns out I was wrong.

I firmly believe that what you find yourself doing in your spare time is the passion you should pursue. Don't *decide* what you want to do with your life; let your life tell you what your path is. That may sound flippant or too easy. And, frankly, it may take years to even figure out your path, much less get your dream job. The key is knowing how to find the clues.

When I look back on my college years, my early career, and even all the way back to my childhood, I realize there were clues all along the way telling me what to do with my life.

THE UNLIKELY EPIPHANY

One night in 1997, my boyfriend, Brian (now my husband), came home with a TV pilot he knew I would love. This new show was going to be the next *Beverly Hills, 90210*, he said. I was a junior in college and I'd never gotten early access to a TV pilot before! But college-dropout Brian had moved to New York to work as "the web guy" at J.Crew's corporate headquarters, and his new employer was dressing the show's cast.

We sat down to watch it that night, and I was not only glued to the screen, I was in tears by the final scene. Admittedly, I'm a sucker for good drama and often shed tears when the writing is intense and the music plays with my emotions. But this time it was different: I was emotional for a whole other reason. At that moment, I had an epiphany. I realized I wanted to work in entertainment. I thought "I want to do that!" I wanted to create content, to decide what would be on TV and when. I didn't know exactly what that job was, I just knew I wanted it.

The show was called *Dawson's Creek*, and I've been an avid fan of that cast, specifically Joshua Jackson, ever since. Basically, *Dawson's Creek* changed my life. Sometimes, the most random and unexpected triggers can lead to huge epiphanies, so if you find yourself getting super emotional about something, pay attention.

PERSONAL PASSIONS + TALENT = WINNING

One thing that's very important—now more than ever—is to remember that it's totally OK not to know. That's the most valuable piece of advice I wish I could give my younger self, especially in my twenties in that after-college uncertainty. It's OK if you don't know what you want to do for a living, or what you want next from your career. It's OK if you aren't sure whether or not you want kids, or even if you don't know what TV show to binge-watch next. It's also OK to change your mind. It's OK if you get accepted into law school and realize after a year that you'd rather work at a nonprofit.

I interview a lot of twentysomethings, and, yes, there are women in their twenties who know exactly what they want to do and are incredibly driven to do it. But they are the minority. Just like those people you hear about who knew at three years old that they wanted to be on a stage or winning gold medals. You think, should I feel like a failure if I don't know this, or if I don't have some incredible talent?

Definitely not. In fact, sometimes people who "know" at an early age still change their minds. So do people who have worked in the same career for twenty years. What matters in your life and what brings you satisfaction can change dramatically over time as your lifestyle evolves, as you master new skills, or as new opportunities present themselves. Especially with the way technology is constantly altering how we live and work, your future dream job might not even be invented yet. As a mother of three girls, I look at my kids and already I'm like, what is their calling? Will they be the star athlete or maybe a musician? A girl who codes or is a scientist? Or something entirely new that I can't predict?

Again, it's OK not to know. Your entire life is about figuring that out, and you may have many different successful careers. Whether you are fifteen, twenty-five, or thirty-five, don't stress. As long as you are trying new things and adapting to the world at large, there is a place for you. Some people just find their place earlier than others.

As a mom, I try not to drive myself nuts figuring out my kids' talents at such a young age. We overschedule our kids these days to expose them to all sorts of activities and help them to figure out what they are interested in. We're helping develop their brains and bodies, but we are also looking for signs. Are they gifted? Do they have a calling? You know what? Most kids don't have a calling. Like you, they are just trying to figure it out. For most of us, these answers come over time.

It's important to play around and discover what turns you on and what gets you excited, because you should probably learn more about whatever it is. Think about what's on the agenda of your best day ever and let that list govern your decisions. Consider both the topics you are passionate about and the activities and tasks that get you excited—like how I love TV and movies but I also enjoy giving advice. The end goal shouldn't be the job your parents want you to have or the job where you think you'll make the most money. Sure, more money makes life easier, but it isn't the only measure of success. There are plenty of uber-rich people who are absolutely miserable. Your goal should be to create the life that's the most satisfying and rewarding to you. If you focus on working hard and following your passion, you will be a more successful and happier person.

THOSE AHA MOMENTS

While I was lucky to have a great childhood and a loving family, my parents also taught me at an early age that nothing comes easy, nor should it. My dad made me get a job every summer throughout high school and college, and my parents always stressed the value of hard work, whether at school, in sports, or at a job.

As a kid, I always tried my hardest, and my teachers saw the effort. What came naturally to me was writing, and I was lucky to have teachers who challenged me to be an even better writer, to be more creative. I can still remember stories and papers I wrote, all the way back to grade school and into high school and college. In elementary school, it was a made-up fish universe with creative names for everything that impressed my teachers. My mind was completely free. The high school story I got the highest grade on was titled—I kid you not—"I Don't Know Yet!" When I finished my neatly typed paper, it was missing only the title. The fact that I didn't overthink it and just hand-wrote those words at the top made my teacher like it even more! My best college paper? When I compared an episode of *The Simpsons* to *Faust*. See what I mean about clues?

I was an avid reader, and I loved escaping into novels. Some days, I wanted to be the next J. D. Salinger or hoped I could write the next big coming-of-age novel. Yet I felt that was a dreamer's paradise. I never thought writing could be a real career. Plus, I was surrounded by people who seemed to have it all figured out: lawyers, doctors, and my super-smart brother. He excelled at math and science, and I knew I wasn't even going to come close there. My BFF is an artist and was even sent to a special school early on to harness that skill. (She's now a talented creative director.)

Me, I just felt lost. I struggled with reading comprehension and was unable to grasp a foreign language (despite really wanting to, even to this day). Once I became interested in psychology, I finally felt like I'd found something that could lead to a career.

ENLIGHTENING YOURSELF

I can't tell you what the perfect intersection of your strengths and passions is. But I can tell you what to look for to find it.

An obvious but incredibly helpful place to start is by

taking a personality test, like Myers-Briggs or DISC or one of hundreds of others that are super easy to find and take online. Even if you think you know everything about yourself, the results will help you think about your talents and interests in new ways. These tests are a great way to expand your thinking and uncover not just the topics that interest you but also the tasks, skills, and activities that make you feel energized.

Also, learn how to take a compliment. When people are saying "thank you" or pointing out how awesome you are at something, take note. It could be that you're good at listening, giving advice, prepping a friend for a job interview, or even being an awesome shopping buddy. Maybe you're persuasive or super organized or good at solving problems. Whatever it is, if you enjoyed spending your time doing this thing someone thinks you are good at, you might be able to turn that strength into a career. Find inspiration in yourself by taking cues from your daily conversations and actions.

Remember your reasons for getting out of bed. Combine your motivation for getting up in the morning with those compliments you're getting to make the blueprint for creating your ultimate dream job. You probably won't get that exact job right away, but you can start by taking baby steps and by getting experience in the industry you want to pursue.

Also, experiment and try new things. As I've said before,

I believe that what you find yourself doing in your spare time can help you find your passion. But that might mean experimenting more with how you spend your spare time and pushing yourself to try something outside your comfort zone. Volunteering can be a great way to discover new skills that you enjoy, as can taking classes. Attend talks and panels by business leaders and see what and who gets you most excited and inspired. Read articles about people and companies, take photos of things that inspire you, and file them away in one spot you can return to.

Keep a journal. Every day (or week or at least month), jot down what made you happy, what you didn't like, or what you got complimented on. Think about what made you happy at work, at school, or outside of work. (You never know who is going to drop out of corporate law to be your next SoulCycle instructor.) Sometimes, it takes a while to acknowledge or recognize what truly makes us happy, but by writing this stuff down, you can read back on it later, notice the patterns, and try to draw conclusions.

Think back to your childhood and try to remember the moments that brought you joy, the things you were obsessed with, and try to figure out what it was about those things that made you so happy. For me, it was soccer, entertainment, and writing. But it could be anything for you!

Then find a way to test out those passions in the real world. Internships and entry-level jobs are valuable for so many reasons. The most obvious benefit is having experience to add to your résumé, but equally important is getting a sense of what it's actually like to work in that industry. You may have your heart set on working in a certain field, only to discover that the work culture doesn't suit you at all or that it doesn't allow for the lifestyle you ultimately want to live. A friend of mine from college was so excited about breaking into the fashion industry, she was willing to do pretty much any task required of her: taking notes for the CEO, fetching coffee, even getting on her knees to clean out a fridge. But in her second gig, after being hit on several times and feeling super uncomfortable, she was strong enough to GTF out. The experience made her realize that as much as she loved fashion, this was not the world she wanted to give her all to, and she found other jobs where she was more appreciated for her mind and her hard work.

On the other hand, you might find that you love the culture but you're not into your day-to-day tasks—the way my internship at FOX helped me realize PR wasn't for me—and the idea of having your boss's job someday seems even less appealing. Those are the passion clues you should take note of. Your early jobs are important not just for the experience but for helping you understand what you *don't* want to do. Don't be too proud to take an internship even after you've graduated from college; they are actually the perfect way to get your foot in the door. Be willing to work at shitty jobs and work hard at them. Nothing should be beneath you. I don't care how big and beautiful the silver spoon in your mouth may be, you can still work at the shittiest job. If you're interested in a certain career path, it's important just to know how things work in that industry and find out if you actually like it. Learn how to be a good coworker, a problem solver, and to support yourself on your own money. From there, figure out what direction to go.

FUEL THE FIRE

By starting POPSUGAR, I guaranteed that I got to do what I loved all day, which was to write, and in the beginning, that was my primary job: writing as much and as fast as I could. But obviously, my role has changed considerably over ten years: I hardly ever have time to write anymore. But I've managed to stay in touch with the passion that inspired us to start POPSUGAR while also discovering new aspects of my job I love just as much.

I miss writing, but I love everything else I get to have my hands in. The first major change in my job description was finding talented people and training them to write in the POPSUGAR voice. Soon, I learned that refining and communicating my vision is a creative endeavor all its own. When we launched POPSUGAR Studios in 2009, my job evolved even more as I learned how to translate written stories into excellent visual narratives on video.

I even found a way to incorporate my love of shopping into my work. I have always loved discovering new brands and products and telling my friends about them, so when we launched the POPSUGAR Must Have box in 2012, it was a natural extension of our editorial vision, not to mention a new revenue source for the company. Although Must Have was never part of the original business plan, I think it has been successful for the same reason POPSUGAR was: because I am truly passionate about doing it. My job now includes testing products, working with a budget, and playing with different themes to create a gift, for yourself or a friend, full of items we recommend. It feels like shopping for all my best friends and it's really fun.

One of my favorite things about my job, though, is hiring new people. Partly it's because I've always trusted my instincts about people but also because I love finding that perfect package: someone with common goals and values who can also introduce me to new areas of interest, whether it's a marketing candidate with incredible experience building brands or a recent college graduate who is obsessed with Snapchat. I love meeting new people who can make up for the strengths that my team and I lack, who can teach me something I keep meaning to learn but haven't gotten around to yet, or who can introduce us to skills we don't even know we need. We move so fast that we get caught up in a million other things, so we need to hire people who lift one another up and help us all become smarter and stronger. Hiring people helps me open my eyes to new cultures, ideas, and ways of thinking, and it makes me happier, too, since new talent often brings new energy to our team, even when we didn't realize we needed it.

I also pay close attention to what our audience and our employees are getting excited about. When we acquired ShopStyle in 2007, it was because Brian saw our editors using the tool. It was an easier way to create wish lists and shopping widgets. Brian reached out to the founders and then again to our editors to find out why we liked it so much. We always knew commerce would play a role in our business, but until we met the ShopStyle team, we weren't sure exactly how. Beyond being a great tool, ShopStyle would let us work directly with retailers, brands, and other media companies who would also want this technology. Nine years later, we're using ShopStyle in ways we could never have imagined.

Through our video team, I found myself in meetings with talent agencies, and during one of our calls, I immediately said I would love a follow-up call with the literary agent. As a brand, I knew we should be publishing books, even if I didn't know what kind of book yet. And here I am, writing a book. In getting back to writing, I've come full circle and reconnected with my original dream.

THE RAINBOW CONNECTION

In any job, staying connected with what you loved in the first place can be a challenge. Taking on more responsibility often means moving further away from the passion that got you there, and you might find you need to reconnect with your roots or find other things you love just as much.

Over the years, we've seen many people at POPSUGAR move from their original roles into completely new ones, whether changing jobs within their department or moving into an entirely different part of the business. Within editorial, we've had a fashion editor move on to the Moms site, a tech editor who decided she'd rather do hard news, and an entertainment editor who became an on-air reporter and then came back to editorial. Even more remarkable are the people who changed departments completely: The editorial director of our Moms site was initially hired to handle our PR, and one of the project managers on our engineering team was also our first food editor. In every case, the employee loved working at POPSUGAR, and we loved having them on the team, so we were more than willing to help them find something new when they needed a change.

It's entirely possible to love your job but still feel incomplete, and if and when that happens to you, it's your job to speak up. But before you do, try to identify what you're struggling with: Are you bored, overwhelmed, or feeling stagnant? From there, consider what changes could actually solve the problem. We want to keep people happy, but that's hard to do unless the person knows what would make them happier. Do you need to adjust the balance in your current job, do you want an entirely new role, or do you want more responsibility?

You can adjust your career path and reconnect with your passions without starting from scratch and abandoning the experience you've worked so hard for. There are a few things you can do, depending on your specific situation, if you feel like something is missing from your job:

1. **Change teams:** We've seen tons of editors who love what they do and can't imagine doing anything else, but they're just a little bored: After writing about the same topic for six years, they just want to write about something else! If you're in a similar situation, think about how you can change the focus of your job without changing the nature of it. From a company perspective, mixing people up every so often is great for innovation and fostering fresh ideas. So look around your department and think about where you'd rather be, then propose the idea to your boss. If you can solve a staffing problem in the process, that's even better.

2. **Change departments:** This is a great option if you love where you work but aren't that into your day-to-day job. When you find a company that feels like a great fit, you hate to leave it! If the feeling is mutual, you company probably doesn't want you to leave either and will be more than willing to find you a new home. I'd much prefer to hold on to someone who already knows the POPSUGAR voice, vision, and values than hire and retrain someone new. So talk to people in other departments and learn more about what they do and what their departments are like. Even if it's a job you've never done before, if you feel excited to try something completely new and it sounds like something you'd be good at, that's a good sign.

3. **Formulate an exit plan:** If you know you've found the career you want, but the place where you work is poison, then please, work on getting out of there! Start reaching out to your contacts and networking ASAP. Learn as much as you can while you wait, but have your résumé ready so you can pounce on similar job openings in a different environment.

Finding what you love is the first step toward creating your dream job, but it isn't the only step. You may find yourself having to reconnect with your passion at different points in your career and adjust your path accordingly. As you become more successful, you'll most likely discover new places where your strengths and passions intersect (and places where they don't). Before we go any further, let's pause and do a little exercise—something you can revisit when you start to feel incomplete, unhappy, or just plain bored.

Answer the following twelve questions as honestly and instinctively as possible, then think about what each answer says about you.

1. When do you feel most energized?
2. What will you wake up early for?
3. What do you stay up late doing?
4. What do you never get sick of talking about?
5. What do you want to spend a chunk of money on?
6. What do your friends come to you for advice on?
7. With friends, are you the one who makes plans or the one who goes along with them?
8. What was your favorite subject in school?
9. What was your favorite extracurricular activity?
10. What extracurricular activity did you try but hate?
11. What weird hobby did you have as a kid?
12. What's one passion or interest you think you could never turn into a job?

CHAPTER 2

EMBARKING ON ADULTHOOD

Pretty much every career starts with a job. The most brilliant talents at the top of their fields started somewhere—and it wasn't the top. Even if your ultimate goal is to be an entrepreneur, it's nearly impossible to come right out of college and start your own company. Whatever your ultimate goal, you need to know an industry inside and out. Want to open a restaurant? Work as a server or a bartender. If you want to break into the fashion industry, get a job in retail. If your goal is directing movies, work as a PA (a production assistant). Journalists usually start out as editorial assistants or researchers, and certified Pilates instructors might have to work the front desk for a while. There is no secret to getting the career of your dreams, but getting a job in the industry is a good place to start.

Of course, getting a job isn't easy, either, and there's no magic formula for landing the job you want. I can't even guarantee that what worked for me will work for you; so much of landing a job is about timing and other factors you can't control. But after ten years spent growing our company and interviewing hundreds of candidates, I can teach you how to master the skills you *can* control: writing a killer e-mail, crafting a résumé that gives you the credit you deserve, networking, nailing an interview, and being persistent without being annoying.

THE SECRET OF MY SORTA SUCCESS

As I began my job search in my last few months of college, I was beyond excited to move to New York City and try to land a job in the entertainment industry. I had no clue beyond my internship at FOX what this entailed, but I was convinced that entertainment was my calling.

I reached out to an old friend who worked at one of the most prestigious talent agencies in the world, and I was thrilled to land an interview. Everyone wore business suits and looked so put together. Even the mailroom attendees looked so chic, and they made only $17,000 a year—oh, and by the way, mailroom was the position I was applying for, since that was the only way in.

I'd romanticized the mailroom a little, because one of my favorite movies growing up was *The Secret of My Success*. In this very 1980s movie, Michael J. Fox plays a young guy from Kansas who moves to New York to strike it rich. After getting a job in the mailroom, he starts posing as a high-powered executive. While I didn't plan to pull off an eighties movie–level caper, I was totally fine starting in the mailroom.

Then I learned there was a minimum of five rounds of interviews and a typing test. OMG. OK. Be patient, I thought, you need to show your commitment to get what you want. Then came some advice from my friend: "Don't wear your engagement ring."

Even now, I know it's not that normal for a twenty-two-year-old to be engaged, especially in New York. I totally get that. But it felt wrong not to be myself, since this was obviously a huge part of who I was and who I still am: super ambitious but equally committed to my marriage and my family.

I made it to round three at the talent agency, which had an intensely hierarchical vibe that reminded me too much of my dad's law firm. When I started my own company seven years later, I still thought about that. I knew I didn't want to create that kind of atmosphere. At the time, I knew I needed to continue to search for jobs elsewhere.

So I started interviewing at a few advertising agencies,

where the atmosphere was way more my style. At one quintessential Madison Avenue agency, Young & Rubicam, I met a team of four smart, ambitious yet sweet women in a single afternoon, and they offered me a job working as a media planner, with Showtime Networks and Sony as my clients. I had twenty-four hours to decide: Take the job in advertising, where I never thought I'd end up, or go back to the cold yet prestigious talent agency, for three more rounds of interviews for the mailroom.

The decision was easy. Even though I'd always thought that working in entertainment was my dream job, I opted for advertising, based on the simple fact that I wanted to work somewhere surrounded by people who seemed creative, smart, and fun. I was able to wear my ring and be myself at that interview, so I felt more at home accepting the position.

I had no idea what working in the ad industry meant when I started, but I really liked the people who hired me. Plus, my clients were tied to entertainment, so I felt I was still on my way to programming network television, my ideal job at that time. The place had a very *Mad Men* feel (except with a lot more women, and without the cool furniture, and with far less exciting wardrobes). You could even smoke if you had a closed door and an open window. Yes, I'm aging myself here, but Philip Morris was one of the company's clients, so maybe we were the end of an era.

My first job post-college was really about signing up to work with people who seemed genuinely interested in my help and input, and in teaching me—well, more like delegating their work to me, but I relished it. It helped me gain confidence to want to grow and learn more.

THE NEED FOR OLD-SCHOOL SOCIAL NETWORKING

"It's all about who you know."

"You need connections."

"Every industry, especially entertainment, is built on nepotism."

"There are about five thousand applicants for the fifteen positions we need to fill each year."

●　●　●

These were the not-so-very encouraging words of advice I heard from friends working in New York when I was trying to land that first job. I felt doomed from the start. I worried that to get anywhere, I was going to have to ask for favors and reach out to friends of friends. While I had a few people to talk to, the list was short. I felt defeated before I even started. How could I do all that hustling and be persistent without pissing everyone off?

Despite my friends' warnings, I learned I didn't need to annoy anyone. I didn't have to have family connections. However, I did have to work harder to build my personal network and learn to strike a balance between persistent and annoying. That meant I did my research and checked job listings often and applied, applied, applied.

Also, I widened my range of fields. When it became clear that entertainment wasn't an easy option, I started to look at advertising, marketing, and PR positions. I made sure to have cover letters that were tailored to each position as much as possible. I learned that when people wanted a position filled, they wanted that person to start ASAP, so letting the hiring manager know I was free right now was key. I would end e-mails with "Looking forward to hearing from you soon"—*soon* being the important word.

Now that I'm on the other side of hiring, I can say that most of these tactics still work, but now we have the added benefit of social media. Finding a friend or a friend of a friend through your socials can also help push a résumé through, so don't hesitate to ask that favor. If your social circles aren't yielding results, consider tapping into your college alumni association or connecting with fellow alums via LinkedIn, Levo League, or whatever is the online networking site of the moment.

Networking is a vague and often terrifying concept, and the need for it never stops, though it means different things at different points in your career. At its most basic, networking, whether in person or online, is a way to get your foot in the door and make a connection with someone in the industry. Once you're in, networking takes different forms. When I was younger, the networking I did took place at my company or at events with other people in the advertising and media world. When you aren't actually looking for a job, networking feels more casual and fun, and it's a great way to learn about the work culture at different companies and how the jobs differ slightly from place to place. You might hear about your peers being promoted quickly (or feeling trapped) or learn about job openings in other companies. Plus, networking when you don't need a job is great practice for when you actually do.

If the idea of attending a networking event terrifies you, you are not alone. We all have moments when we feel awkward and insecure. Talking to complete strangers can be incredibly uncomfortable—for everyone!—but like any other skill, it gets easier the more you do it. Try to ease yourself in. Before you throw yourself into a massive industry event or an unfamiliar environment, practice stepping out of your comfort zone in small ways: Talk in the office kitchen to a coworker you haven't met before, volunteer to deliver a presentation to a small group, or attend that after-work happy hour you usually skip. By forcing yourself to talk to your coworkers more, you'll start to learn how to socialize in a professional setting.

It really helps to find a networking buddy. When I am at industry events or other places where my peers are, I am eager to find someone I relate to and can partner with for the remainder of the event. From there, we join forces and meet even more people. Afterward, I always try to send a note or connect on social to help myself remember these great people when we cross paths again. You never know when you might want to reach out about a job, get details about a new coworker, or just talk to a peer who is facing challenges similar to yours.

At this point in my life, networking is mostly about meeting interesting people doing interesting things and seeing if and how we can do them together. Other times, it's refreshing to meet another person dealing with the same work/life challenges I'm trying to balance. In fact, I often turn down networking events, but I still make sure to go to events or conferences where everyone will be, and I enjoy the quality time away from the office, the daily routine, and the usual distractions. It's worth it to get a new tip about hiring the next generation or to learn about a new delivery service for dinner or a cool app that helps me organize my to-do lists. When friendships develop, it can lead to business partnerships, investments, press opportunities, or being referred to great candidates—who knows?

When you meet someone in your field who you connect with, whether it's at an industry event or a friend's cocktail party, take notes. I will admit, remembering names is not my specialty, especially after interviewing hundreds of people over the past ten years, which is enough to challenge even the best memory. When I would interview candidates before social media existed, I'd take notes about what they looked like or what they were wearing, just to jog my memory later. Now, I can look them up on Facebook or Instagram, but I still take notes out of habit.

If you think you might want to reach out later, ask for a business card and then jot down a few details on the back about what you talked about or anything else to help you remember them later. I don't carry business cards myself, but this is one of the things I'm always trying to work on! You can also take notes on your phone or, if you get a phone number, use the NOTES feature in your contacts. I will also e-mail myself with all this information so I have it in my in-box anytime. Anything works, but try to do it as soon as possible after the conversation. I am always wowed when someone remembers me from the one-off place we met or the specifics of our conversation. That's a perfect example of how to make an impression without being annoying.

When you find a contact who might be able to help, don't be afraid to take a chance and send her an e-mail, even if she's a total stranger. If possible, ask your mutual acquaintance to introduce you over e-mail or for permission to mention her name in your own e-mail to the contact. Most likely the worst that can happen is that no one writes you back.

That said, there is a right way and wrong way to reach out to busy people, and your primary goal should be to not waste a second of anyone's time. The quicker and cleaner the e-mail, the higher the likelihood this helpful stranger will read it. Be friendly yet professional, check for errors before you hit SEND, be direct about what you're asking, and don't ramble. Make sure the e-mail is short and sweet but also contains information that will make the person want to react. Be direct about what you are interested in up front. Don't ask the CEO for coffee or even an informational meeting. Don't ask how to land a job at that company, or other vague questions you could answer on your own, like how the company got started (Google it! It's most definitely already out there). Instead, state your interest, show some personality, and imply that you are open to being passed along to whoever would be the best person to follow up with.

Also, remember that you need to stand out from the e-mail clutter, and giving your message a creative subject line can help. Something like "For your consideration: the perfect candidate for XYZ." Or craft something specific to the company, such as:

- 8 reasons I'd be great for a job at POPSUGAR
- Social media addict at your service
- Matt Damon is my #1, too

Or you can just be super straightforward with some connection: friend of your mom, college roommate, GW alum for hire, went to Camp Teen Town also!, etc.

Getting someone's attention can be hard, so knowing the right time to send an e-mail is important. Everyone has their own routines, so try to predict what might be the busiest and least likely times to get someone's attention. Typically, earlier in the week or first thing in the morning is not a good time; and by Friday afternoon, people want to check out. Look for a sweet spot of downtime, maybe during lunch or the early afternoon. Also, keep in mind whatever is going on in their world at the time: E-mailing a fashion editor during Fashion Week or an ad sales exec at the end of the fiscal year is not going to work.

Once that e-mail is sent, wait. Please, please don't bombard your potentially golden contact with countless follow-up e-mails, because while finding a job is your first priority, you are not hers. I really do want to help all of the young, talented, hardworking women and men who are just starting out—after all, I remember what it was like not to know anyone—but while giving advice is one of the most fulfilling aspects of my job, it is sadly also the least urgent task on most days. Resist the urge to follow up if you get antsy two days later—and definitely don't start e-mailing a bunch of people at the same company trying to track down more help. You can attempt to bubble yourself back up in their head by following them on social media, but don't e-mail them, send a LinkedIn message, and start tweeting at them at all once. That is a turnoff.

If you haven't heard back in a week or two, it's safe to

send a polite nudge in case your e-mail was overlooked or forgotten despite the best intentions, and don't be surprised if you eventually get a very belated response. ;) Make three attempts, max, then move on and don't take it personally. It drives me nuts when, after three attempts, I get an e-mail saying, "I know you're really busy, so you probably missed my earlier e-mails." Because while I do miss e-mails, if I haven't responded by the third pass, chances are it's not the right time or the right fit and it's time to move on for now.

So what makes me more likely to respond to someone? When he or she comes across as creative and genuine and has something to show for themselves, I am interested. When someone creates a connection back to the site, especially something specific, such as "I've watched all of your food videos and totally made that supersize Oreo for a party," I know they are familiar with what we do and also connect with it. If you're looking for a job in editorial, I love seeing that someone has a real interest in our content, and I'd imagine it's the same anywhere. If you were trying to land a job at J.Crew, you might talk about a favorite item of clothing you still have ten years after buying it, or how Jenna Lyons inspired your glasses style. Or make a connection between the job you're after and those childhood interests; tell a story from when you were younger that, looking back, you realize was a sign. Just try not to go overboard; if someone is too much a fangirl, I get a little worried that this job could never live up to her fantastical expectations.

Sometimes, timing is everything, and other times, it's about the person, so keep an eye out for staff changes. I often deal with this working on the Must Have box. We've reached out to a brand because we want to include them in a monthly box, but the contact at the time doesn't think it's a good fit or can't make it work. But we don't give up: We often go back to brands when they have someone new in place, because so much of getting hired or partnering with another company is about finding someone who gets your vision. Over the years, I've seen the same people apply for more than one job at POPSUGAR, and sometimes it makes sense. But if we see the same name apply for every job we have open, it can start to look desperate. It's important to recognize when something isn't connecting for a reason, especially when you haven't even gotten to the interview stage. But rather than let it bum you out, use it as a clue to help figure out what might be holding you back and what you really want to do.

Just as every career starts with a job, every job search begins with a résumé. The formats vary slightly from industry to industry, so do some research and find out what's expected in your field. That said, some rules apply no matter the situation: A good résumé should be free of errors, honest and accurate, and as clear and easy to digest as possible. Ask a friend (or two) to read over your résumé, then double- and triple-check everything yourself as well. Make every word count by avoiding clichéd adjectives like *flexible* and *creative*.

The unfortunate truth is that the résumé you worked so hard on will usually be scanned by someone in ten seconds or less, and one error could turn them off entirely.

Though the days of printing out a hard copy of your résumé on fancy paper are behind us, that doesn't give you permission to make your résumé two (I've even seen three) pages when you're just starting your career. Editing smartly will show you in a better light. Don't be tempted to list every single responsibility you had at every former job—just the most relevant quick hits and measurable successes. I also prefer a résumé that's specific and relevant to the job. There's no reason to include ALL of your unrelated job experience unless it's to serve a specific purpose, like filling in gaps that might raise questions—though we love seeing your volunteer experience! Also, steer clear of using a generic file name like "resume" and instead make sure the document name contains your first and last name; that makes it much easier for me to find when I'm searching for it later.

Even in the digital age, don't underestimate the importance of your first piece of communication: what we still call a cover letter (but probably not for long). While your résumé proves that you are qualified for a job, the cover letter is your chance to give potential employers a glimpse at your personality and set yourself apart from applicants who are equally qualified. Unless the job listing instructs otherwise, don't attach the cover letter as a separate doc; just write it in the body of an e-mail. For length, aim for somewhere between a traditional cover letter and a networking e-mail—two to three solid paragraphs. And even if you've sent the same note to other potential employers, don't let it sound that way. Double- and triple-check your writing—especially the variables that you edit each time, like the name of the company or hiring manager. Your résumé could be sparklingly brilliant, but if the body of your e-mail is addressed to the wrong person, it might not even make it past the first set of eyes.

INTERVIEWING AND FAILING (AND WHY THAT'S OK)

Looking for jobs was way harder fifteen years ago. We did a lot of "informational interviews," which meant you weren't interviewing for a specific job, just making connections and learning about a company. You didn't really know what a job was until you went to talk to someone who did it.

With the Internet, informational interviews are becoming a thing of the past. There is a ridiculous amount of information out there if you want to find it; you can research pretty much any type of job online, find out what it pays, and learn about the day-to-day responsibilities. You can even read reviews about specific companies written by past and current employees. The Internet makes it insanely easy to deep-dive into different industries and companies, and as a result, people are far less willing to spend time on informational interviews—especially with someone who doesn't have any experience or connections.

I recommend getting as much as you can out of the company you work for. Whether you're an intern who's still in college or a veteran considering a career change, chances are there is someone at your company who can and will be happy to offer some insight, so find the person whose job is closest to the job you think you want and ask for a quick, informal meeting. Most people are far more willing to spend fifteen or thirty minutes chatting with a colleague than with a complete stranger, and even if they can't help you, they probably know someone who can. For instance, say you work at a nonprofit and you think your true calling is investment banking; it can't hurt to reach out to someone in the accounting department and pick her brain. She might know someone else in the finance world for you to reach out to and give you a better sense of the culture. It works the other direction, too: If you work in investment banking, try to find the coworker who used to be in nonprofits. So many people change careers these days, you never know who might be a great resource until you ask around.

Just make sure you do your research first. Because there is so much information available online, your first stop shouldn't be an informational interview or even a casual conversation. Don't waste someone's time asking basic questions you could answer on your own. It drives me nuts when someone says, "I want to talk to you about how to get into online media," and asks me for advice on where to start. Not only because I'm too busy to map out someone else's career path, but also because doing your research shows that you are both resourceful and committed. When you meet people working in what seem like jobs you want, ask them specific questions only they can answer: What's your typical day like? What do you love most about this job? How has your job changed since you started here? What surprised you most?

When I graduated from college, I hated the idea of taking an unpaid internship after spending so much money on an education. But as frustrating as it sounded, I interviewed at plenty of places that offered unpaid internships and I was pretty close to taking one. I know many successful people who interned for free, often working part-time jobs on the side. Looking back, I realize it's not much different from what I did when I started POPSUGAR while working a full-time job. Plus, the earlier you do it, the faster you can figure out if it's what you want and if you're actually good at it. Just as at a job, you'll learn what parts you like and don't like, and where your passion intersects with your strengths. Whatever new skills you learn in the process will make you even more hirable, and more confident.

When I was younger—in my teens and twenties—I probably cared too much about what people thought of me. I wasn't as confident speaking up in school and, later, in meetings at work. But with my friends, when I was comfortable, I could barely shut up. I never felt that way at work until I started POPSUGAR. POPSUGAR made me comfortable; having an outlet to write gave me more confidence to keep writing. I felt I could be myself, even though it wasn't all about me. While I shared some personal stuff on POPSUGAR in the early days, like the fact that I was pregnant or my opinion on specific topics, it was never a personal blog. I didn't include the daily diary-like details like most blogs that started at the same time. It was what I had to say, and finding common ground with my readers, that brought people back to the site. While it's important to find friends who like you for who you are, loving what you do and having people appreciate what you're doing fosters an entirely different type of confidence.

Pursuing your passion on the side can help you build the reassurance you need to turn that passion into a job. As you become an expert, stay active on social media and show that you're knowledgeable about a subject. Think of it as an add-on to the official experience you list on your résumé. Actually, one of the first things I do before or after interviewing candidates for jobs at POPSUGAR is check out their social media accounts; it's a great way to get a sense of someone's personality, humor, writing talent, and aesthetics. I can feel out whether or not they'd be a good fit for the job and our company—or at least get a look inside what motivates and moves them. This doesn't mean you have to hold back on bachelorette party pictures or having an epic night out. As long as you keep it PG-13, I want to see you hanging with your friends, your dog, your latte art, etc. I like seeing that you are a Harry Potter devotee or a Star Wars fanatic, or both. I appreciate if you do or don't dress up on Halloween or document your Sunday brunch. I can start to see pieces of your personality, whether you value alone time, have a sweet tooth, are an extreme extrovert, or an animal lover. The captions you write, the products you like, and the people you surround yourself with give a potential coworker an inside look at who you really are—things I might not figure out during a job interview but love to know because they make you more human. The problem with job interviews is that they can only tell me so much; I can get a glimpse of someone's personality, but only to a point. Don't get me wrong: After years of interviewing hundreds of candidates, I can tell pretty quickly if you're a good fit, but social media gives me a fuller picture, so make sure yours reflects who you are and how you want to be seen.

Pursuing a job in entertainment right out of college, I learned it was a lot about who you knew, and many people wanted me to work for free. Even some of the coolest jobs that pay no money are the hardest to get, with hundreds of people going after the same opportunities you are. Chances are, you'll be rejected from a few places before you get hired, and it's going to suck. You'll even be rejected from jobs you know you're qualified for, when you know you nailed the interview. Those rejections can make you doubt yourself and wonder if you are on the right path.

As someone who has interviewed hundreds of people over the past ten years, I can tell you that plenty of candidates are rejected even when they are totally qualified, very impressive, and highly talented. Most of the time, if you even make it to the interview stage, you are qualified. Someone else might be just a little bit more qualified or a slightly better fit. There are a million factors that go into hiring people.

As much as you can help it, don't worry about being rejected for a job—you have a goal and you shouldn't lose sight of it! When you do hear from the hiring manager delivering the sad news, tell her that you're disappointed and really hoped it would work out and to please keep you on file for possible openings in the future. We do that at POPSUGAR: There are many people who leave a lasting impression but just didn't work for that particular day/job/team. So don't take it too personally. Eventually, you will find a job.

POPSUGAR, THEN AND NOW

Writing was so easy in the beginning. When I first started writing POPSUGAR in 2005, everything just poured out of me. I couldn't type fast enough, always found stories, and never felt there was a slow day. The pre–social media and post–blog world was also spinning in the best way possible. Readers loved that we could now see so much more of celebrities than when we only had weekly magazines. Every event with a red carpet became an opportunity to share some great outfit, a new couple, or a rising star, and traffic was exploding quickly.

By June 2006, we had built our founding team: me, Brian, Arthur Cinader Jr. and Brian Dhatt (engineers), Tabetha Hinman (lawyer/HR), Krista Moatz (managing editor), and, shortly later, Jason Rhee (business development). Krista, a good friend of mine, quickly morphed into a jack-of-all-trades, from handling finance and office operations to staffing and training our editorial team. When we got funding in September, that meant a lot less writing and a lot more recruiting and training, and the pattern continued—except now I do even more: developing video concepts, reviewing scripts, and working with sales and marketing on our shared vision.

We decided early on to create different websites for different categories, starting with advice, fashion, beauty, food, and fitness. As much as I loved to write, as I did in school, I was not a great speller, and grammar became an afterthought. I was more focused on establishing a voice that was casual, carefree, and felt as if you were having a conversation with a friend. But I wanted to hire experienced journalists, too, both to fill the gaps in my knowledge and to educate me in the process. I needed people who had gone to journalism school and I wanted to learn more about it myself (without having to actually go back to school). So I prioritized hiring smart people who were gleeful grammar geeks and who understood the importance of a strong lede. I also wanted to find people who had passion, who were smart, motivated, and liked the same things I did. I was addicted to using analytics to study traffic, and I wanted our new hires to have the same obsession, so it was important to me to train people on these tools and empower them to use them.

Rather than do everything myself, I learned to solidify a creative vision and communicate it to everyone else; it's something we still do today, as we all learn and grow together. While I'm not the strongest writer on the team, I do have strong opinions and a creative vision that allows me to give lots of editorial direction even when I'm not writing. Now it's my responsibility to keep my voice heard without slowing down the teams, while also allowing new voices to be introduced and adapted.

Running a team requires learning when to delegate and how much and when to let go. Letting go can be the harder part for some leaders. Especially if you love what you do, you want to stay connected, but the way you grow is to know when to let go! Once we find great people to hire, we are more than happy to train them (very intensely) and then hand things off once trust is in place, though training is an ongoing process: We are constantly retraining people, sending feedback, creating guidelines, you name it.

HOW TO EXPAND YOUR ROLE

Finding a career that you love and you're good at is no easy feat. Some people never experience it. Often, once you find it, you just want more; it's only natural when you find a fulfilling job at a company you love to start thinking about next steps and how to expand your role. Own it. Think big. Be ambitious. Just don't lose sight of what makes you happy. Do what you want to do, not what you think you should do. That's true of choosing a career but also true of shaping a career.

Before you start asking for promotions or more responsibility, think about what you really want out of your career or what you want it to look like. Being ambitious for ambition's sake can lead to trouble down the line. Instead, focus on strategic ambition, which is much better for you in the long run and also far more appealing to employers. Ask yourself, Do I want my boss's job someday, or my boss's boss's job? If not, where do I see myself in two years? Trust your gut: If the thought of having your boss's job makes you cringe, then that might not be the path for you. If you find yourself gravitating toward responsibilities at the next level, chances are, you want to move up at the organization.

If you feel you're ready, start by asking for more responsibility before you come right out and ask for a promotion. By volunteering to take on new tasks and projects, you prove to your manager that you're capable of handling a larger role. But beware of being overeager and volunteering for anything and everything. Instead, be strategic about what you volunteer for; focus on the responsibilities you think you will enjoy and excel at. Recognizing your own strengths, weaknesses, likes, and dislikes is crucial if you want to grow within a company. Identify three to five areas in which you want to become an expert, with the ultimate goal of making yourself indispensable and your promotion inevitable. Not only will this help you craft the career path you want, but it will also allow you to shine. You'll be happier in the long run, because you'll have a job where your passions intersect with your strengths.

When it comes to promotions, there is a perception that you have to pay your dues, put in the time, and "earn it" in order to get ahead. In some industries, that is absolutely the case. But most of the time, it's more complex than that. We want you to show that you understand and want the job by proving you can do it. We want to see you master every aspect of your current job so that moving up is inevitable. You don't deserve more responsibility purely because you have put in the time.

Whether you're looking for a job or gunning for a promotion, this questionnaire can help you answer the all-important question: Are you ready to take the next step?

● ● ●

1. Have you done your research about the job or company?
2. Is your résumé up-to-date *and* proofread?
3. Is your résumé reflective of your greatness and the best practices?
4. Do you have a list of people to contact?
5. Have you researched the field you want to work in?
6. Do you have a list of killer questions to ask in an interview?
7. Are your social media accounts PG-13 and reflective of your talents?
8. Where do you see yourself in two years?

CHAPTER 3

JUST DO IT

Just thinking about making a major change in life can be absolutely terrifying—whether it's moving across the country, enrolling in grad school, breaking up with someone, or buying your first house. But even scarier is making a major change in your career, because wrapped up in the fear is uncertainty about your paycheck. It's much easier to be certain when something is wrong; when a relationship has run its course or it's time to leave a job, the signs are pretty hard to ignore. Knowing when something is right is more of a challenge, and you can't know how it's all going to work out until you do it. Just be sure that when you take that leap, you do so with the right amount of caution.

THE GENESIS OF POPSUGAR

You've read a lot about how POPSUGAR became my passion, but the story of how it became a business is just as important to me. It all started on the cusp of 2005; I remember talking to a girlfriend on New Year's Eve, saying I couldn't believe there wasn't one magazine or website right for a girl like me. Someone who wanted real-time celebrity news, fashion, beauty, a little *Real Simple*, some *Oprah*, great advice, tips, and some humor.

A few months later, Brian and I were hanging out with our new friend Om Malik and discussing the exact same thing, but this time Brian was helping Om with his website. Om was an old-school journalist who saw a big bright future in online writing. He listened to me talk about what I still considered useless knowledge, but instead of dismissing me, he urged me to start writing. As a writer and tech entrepreneur himself, he knew I wanted to create content but that I was struggling to figure how and where. His response? Just have your husband build you a website, learn some simple coding, and start writing. Simple. Just start doing it.

So I did. I didn't even tell my friends at first. I wanted to force myself to get into a groove. I wanted to develop the healthy habit of writing every day. The same way I had throughout my life in a journal, but this time, the writing wasn't about me or my day; it was about things I loved that I was observing, curating, craving, and creating content around. I started off writing about whatever excited me the most: reviews of shows, books, and magazine articles, stories about new beauty products or a purse I wanted. The same stuff I'd been telling my friends about for years. I set small goals that were attainable and satisfying, like writing two kinds of stories each day: one review of an article, show, or story, and the other a list of links to the must-read stories I felt people needed to know. Hitting that goal every day gave me a sense of accomplishment and made me feel I was working toward my goal of creating content, even if no one was paying me to do it.

Although POPSUGAR started as a side project, I soon became addicted to it in a way that I'd never felt at a job. Very quickly, people started discovering the site. I knew that the more I posted, the more people would come back, because that's what *I* wanted as a reader. I craved the instant feedback, which was completely novel to me. In advertising, unless we were buying lots of TV, we didn't get to see such immediate results; it was difficult to correlate how much spending money on magazine ads led people to book a cruise. Now, I could actually see what people were reacting to in real time, and it became hard to tear myself away from the computer. I would write before bed while I watched TV. I would write as part of my morning routine, without being late to my real job. Lunch break, throw up a story. Weekends, why wait? Anything I found exciting, I tried my hardest to get up immediately.

Gradually, it started to morph into an obsession with finding and discovering stories before anyone else did. I wanted to train people to come to POPSUGAR first, and I learned that speed was of the utmost importance. I found sites that had celebrity photos no one had seen yet, and because I knew I was excited to see them, I started sharing them—all with the fun, friendly voice that would come to define POPSUGAR. Thanks to my advertising job, I got my hands on magazines early, and I'd share the highlights from my favorite articles online even before the magazines did. Meanwhile, my addiction to writing kept getting more and more intense. Naturally, POPSUGAR's first tagline was "Insanely Addictive."

Although I had told a few people here and there, I finally told my friends and my parents what I was doing, but it probably took almost six months for me to fully reveal what I'd been up to. It was easier to explain to newer friends who didn't know me as well and who lived in San Francisco and understood how the technology and media space was erupting. Some of those friends happened to be in PR and helped get me access to movie screenings. They also became some of my very early supporters and cheerleaders and told all their friends in the industry to read POPSUGAR. The audience was far beyond the number of people I knew personally, and things were taking off. It was time to go all in.

CREATING YOUR OWN OPPORTUNITY

If you think you've figured out what kind of work you find addictive, don't wait for someone to hire you to do it. Just do it. If you want to be a food writer, start your own food blog. If you want to be a photographer, build an Instagram following. Don't worry about "not having time," because if you love doing it, you will find the time. Think about it: People with full-time jobs find time for their hobbies. Someone who loves softball finds time to play in a league. Aspiring novelists write in their spare time, and musicians have band practice on weekends. Sometimes they're hoping to make a living at it, and sometimes they aren't, but the end result is the same: prioritizing something that makes them happy. They just do it.

Of course, that's easier said than done. It wasn't easy for me, either—I didn't find my passion until I'd been out of college for seven years. But I want everyone to be able to get to the same place and find a job that they love. To do that, you have to be willing to pursue your passions and take risks when the time is right. Understand, it won't necessarily be an easy journey, and it won't happen right away. But just knowing what you want to do and what you don't is the first step.

While I give my dad a lot of credit for my work ethic, I also owe a great deal to my mom. Aside, of course, from giving me the greatest gift of all—life on this planet—she taught me the power of just doing and knowing when to reconnect with what makes you you. Before my brother and I were born, my mom worked as a buyer in fancy retail stores until opting to stay home to raise us. But as soon as she recognized that she needed something else to feel complete, she just did it. Her priority wasn't to make as much money as possible or pick up her career where she left off. To feel happy and more fulfilled, she needed a job to go to every day and the comfort of making her own money. So when I was in middle school, she went back to work teaching knitting. She loved being able to teach other people something she loved and having an outlet to create clothes (and so many blankets). When knitting was no longer an option, she went to work in a cute boutique with trendy clothes (which was great for me, since the clothes were more suited for my age group than for hers, which meant lots of discounts on designer jeans and tees).

At various stages in life, you will need to check your ego at the door. Whether you're just out of college, quitting a job to pursue a passion, making a radical career change, or returning to work after having kids, you have to start somewhere, and there is usually a learning curve. Even if you were the smartest, prettiest, most popular kid in school, at some point in your life, you'll be a beginner. Same goes for making a career change; even if you have twenty years of work experience, you will have a lot to learn with each new challenge. Returning to work after raising kids or taking maternity leave requires lots of catching up and getting up to speed again. But the best way to learn something new is to do it.

The key is making sure you actually do it. We all know people who have been talking about the novel they want to write for years without putting any words to paper. My advice: Set those small, attainable goals for yourself that you can achieve even in your spare time. Hold yourself accountable, and keep track of what you're doing and learning in the process. Some of the lessons from POPSUGAR's early days—like the importance of speed and staying true to our unique voice—still shape the decisions I make today. Keeping track of whether you are hitting your goals also helps you stay honest with yourself. If you find yourself never making time for the thing you're supposed to be "just doing," it might mean your goals are too lofty, but it might also mean that this isn't the thing you're actually meant to do.

If you feel truly passionate about something—regardless of your situation—I promise, you can just start doing it. POPSUGAR became successful because I was eating, sleeping, and dreaming about it nonstop. I could work all night and on the weekends when most other sites were done for the day. You, too, might have to make sacrifices and devote less time to other things, like cooking dinner or going to the gym or going on dates or even hanging out with friends.

Sometimes, it feels as though you have two jobs, and it sucks. But if you do it right, the sacrifice will be only temporary, and it will pay off when your side project turns into a full-time gig.

One of my favorite movies is *Almost Famous,* partly because the main character, William Miller, is the embodiment of "just do it." At fifteen, he gets a gig writing for *Rolling Stone;* he's so into music that he can't imagine doing anything else. But I also absolutely adore what his sister says, when she runs into him after he's spent months doing what he loves: "You look awful, but it's great. You're living your life."

FINDING YOUR PERSONAL PLAN

I don't believe in having a "five-year-plan." Clearly, I never had one until I decided to devote myself to POPSUGAR full-time. When I took the job at Showtime, I knew it wasn't much different from my job at Y&R, but it was getting me closer to my goal. When I moved to San Francisco, a job at a local magazine could have moved me toward my writing goal, but I wasn't passionate about creating that kind of content. Now, I am often asked about POPSUGAR's five-year-plan as a company. We understand the need to see the long-term path, but I also can't predict the future and there are so many unknowns. Same goes for careers. All you can do is have an idea of what you want to be doing in five years, whether it's specific, such as being the editorial director of a beauty website, or as broad as being excited to come to work every day. Also, be prepared to rethink that five-year vision: Your goal is likely to change and evolve over the years, as you get a better sense of your strengths and weaknesses, as you discover new jobs you didn't even know existed, or as your priorities shift in terms of money, family, and work/life balance. The ideal combination of passion + strengths + ultimate goal will be different and evolving for every person. But let your ideal combination govern your decision making.

Remember, whether you're breaking into a field or changing careers, you should be willing to start at the bottom. One of our star employees at POPSUGAR started as an executive assistant. Lizzy Eisenberg wasn't sure what she wanted to do, but she was willing to do everything and learn anything. While she was great at scheduling calendars, booking travel, and setting up board meetings, Brian and I quickly saw her other strengths: never taking no for an answer, enjoying a challenge, and finding alternate solutions to problems. She also has an incredibly inviting personality that makes everyone smile. Over the years, she's advanced through various roles and is now director of business development for ShopStyle.

You have to put in the work and be grateful for the learning experience, because even if you think you are too good for certain jobs and tasks, you can always find something to take away from it. If you want to break into the fashion industry, get a job in retail. While fashion design requires a whole other set of skills, you can still apply what you have learned about bestselling products, fit, color, style, and so on. If you dream of opening your own restaurant, do not be too proud to do a tour of duty as a server or maître d'. If you're really talented, you'll probably get to skip a few steps on the way to your dream job, but I think it's incredibly valuable to understand how an industry works. Folding jeans and fetching props is an education all its own, because it allows you to watch and learn, to get a sense of the culture in that industry, see if employees at your company seem happy or miserable, and find out how the people above you broke into this field. You learn the detailed operations and might even see areas where companies can evolve their practices. You get to know the industry in a way you couldn't on the outside, and you might uncover related industries that could be an even better fit for you.

Before making a change in your career, think about what it is you really want from work. When my mom went back to work after having kids, she just wanted a job to go to that made her happy. Most of us need a paycheck; it definitely isn't cheap to live in a big city, have a family, go to concerts, take vacations—even going to the movies is expensive. But it's up to you to decide how to balance the money you need with what makes you happy and keeps your mind and body healthy. If you've decided it's time to take a break from your career to pursue a passion—like writing a novel or starting a business—your challenge will be not only money but also finding the perfect timing for you, your career, and your personal life.

NEW PASSIONS AND TINY TRIUMPHS

In the case of POPSUGAR, starting at the bottom meant doing it on my own and on the side, and I learned so much in the process. I discovered new passions and tiny triumphs that I would never have found had I not just started doing it. I loved the search for the story. I was constantly going down rabbit holes to be the first to see what celebrity was where and what they were doing. Beating the big guys was the best! My routine of waking up early to write and staying up super late got more and more intense. I found breaks throughout the workday, let myself order takeout instead of cooking, skipped the gym or a phone call from Mom (sorry, Mom!) if I had to. The site started consuming my social life, too: I would tell friends I was going to be late or maybe not even go out, and I rudely had my computer out when we had company over to hang. Basically, any spare second, if there was something to write, I was on my computer.

As a result, the POPSUGAR audience was exploding. I was driven to keep creating this site I knew could be far bigger than me. After six months as a side project, POP-SUGAR had grown so much that I realized it was time to do this full-time. So in November 2005, I quit my job and never looked back.

Oh, and I also found out I was pregnant.

That family I wanted to start was about to happen, and I'd found a job that was making me very little money but was energizing me like nothing had before. I had some small checks coming in from ad-serving agencies, but I didn't want to muck up the site with lots of ads, and it definitely wasn't enough to live on anyway, especially in San Francisco. While I wasn't making much money, I wanted to make traffic skyrocket. I would work in pj's, writing from the minute I got up until I forced myself to take a break. I did have dogs, so that got me out of the house for at least fifteen minutes in the morning and afternoon, though poor Jack and Lucy often had to wait until I got a story up. Because I was pregnant, I wanted to make sure I was moving my body and keeping my mind clear, so I tried hard to get to the gym almost every afternoon. I also had a favorite lunch spot where I'd often eat by myself and take a magazine so I could read something not on a computer screen (but still not unrelated to what I was writing). I would get dinner ready for Brian and me, since he was still dealing with his crappy long commute, and I wanted to be the awesome wife who was doing something useful. :) From November through the New Year, I worked nonstop; Brian saw the traffic numbers making a beautiful hockey-stick graph and decided it was time to join me and make POPSUGAR his next venture.

We incorporated POPSUGAR in April 2006, and within a few months, we started hiring people to help me out, since I was working day and night and about to have a baby. Suddenly, that thing I was "just doing" was very, very real. We had our first six hires over to our house for training on June 1—the precise day that Katie chose to arrive, two weeks early. She was born on a Thursday, and by Sunday, I was back online, covering the MTV Movie Awards.

Going into labor is one of those days I will never forget for a million reasons, but one thing that sticks with me is the loyal POPSUGAR audience wondering where I was. In the past, I'd occasionally let people know when I was taking a day off or traveling (pre-Internet on planes—remember those days?). But when, without warning, the large number of postings I'd normally do was suddenly absent, the readers began leaving comments wondering what was going on. Once I actually decided I was in labor—I was in such denial that I was blaming my bad stomach cramps on a hot dog at the Madonna concert the night before!—I posted that the baby was on the way and I would be back soon. My new blogger friends who linked to POPSUGAR daily were cheering me on, so it was a relief that I had not let anyone down. That said, I felt so dedicated to my audience that I couldn't wait to get back to work as soon as I could!

It might sound silly that I was covering an event a few days later, but babies sleep a lot and I felt a strong responsibility to get back to what was making me (and, I'd like to believe, the audience) so happy!

TURNING EARLY SUCCESS INTO THE REAL THING

I love being "in it." At POPSUGAR, I want our leaders to know how to do the jobs everyone on their team is doing. Partly because we believe that the managers should be able to switch gears from thinking about the big picture to getting their hands dirty in the minute details; it's the only way to stay connected to what's really driving the business. But on another level, I think that reconnecting with the passion that inspired your "just do it" moment keeps your job feeling fun, engaging, and rewarding in the months and years to come. Even as we lead a company of nearly five hundred employees, Brian still codes when he can, and I still get online to cover every award show, join brainstorms, and analyze data daily. Our most senior editors write when inspiration strikes, and daily when the team needs support. In other departments, engineers are constantly learning new coding languages; at our video studios, the producers not only know how to make something beautiful to watch but also how to write stories. It reminds us what we're asking of our employees, and it's also a great source of in-spiration and innovation.

Brian and I haven't let go of our "just do it" philosophy. We never hesitate to act on promising ideas or expand into new businesses we believe in. But that only works if we can admit when something isn't working and acknowledge that we don't have all the answers. Whether you're the CEO or an intern right out of college, it's important to stay humble and remember that you always have more to learn. Even if you've been "just doing it" for years, don't ever assume that you know all there is to know, because you simply don't. The more successful POPSUGAR becomes, the more I'm for-tunate to meet talented people who know more than I do or who have completely different skills from mine. Although my priorities have shifted from creating my dream job to creating a successful and secure company, I haven't stopped thinking about what comes next.

Questions to ask yourself before you just do it

- What is the one thing I wish I could change about my job?

- The most important person I can learn from right now is _____.

- What job or industry do I see myself working in five years from now?

- Who can I talk to in my professional network to learn more about it?

- Is now the time for a career change? If not, how can I start "just doing it" on the side?

- What mini goal will I accomplish each day or week?

- I will record my progress by _____.

- What have I learned since starting? What surprised me?

- Is my five-year vision the same, or has it changed? If it has changed significantly, start this exercise again from the beginning. If it's the same, outline the next five steps I can take to get there.

CHAPTER 4

WORK HARD, PLAY NICE

"Work hard, play nice" is my mantra. I learned it growing up, and now I want my children to live and breathe it. No one deserves good things in life if they cheat their way to get there. One thing I knew for sure when I became "the boss" (though I hate that word and try to never use it) is that I never wanted to be intimidating. I wanted to encourage people to work hard and find their strengths without resorting to scare tactics. Thankfully, it's working for me: "Work hard, play nice" has become my overarching philosophy in life and in work. After all, we all knew the mean girl in high school or the bitch in the office, but I didn't want to play dirty with them. I believe that playing nice will get you just as far—as long as you work hard. Nice girls can be badasses, too, without being bitches.

WTF DOES "WORK HARD, PLAY NICE" MEAN?

When I first started POPSUGAR, my mission was to create a website that would be a refreshing break from all the snarkiness and meanness on the Internet; at the time, there just wasn't a fun, friendly, safe place for content online. For me, *nice* doesn't mean saccharine or relentlessly positive. It can mean being fiercely competitive (which I'll be the first to admit I am) as long as you play by the rules. Nor does *nice* mean being sickly sweet or timid (I also curse like a sailor). My brand of nice comes from a place of honesty, supporting others, and being empathetic. *Nice* is the simple lesson you learn in preschool: Do unto others as you would have them do unto you. I cannot stand anyone who acts like an asshole to flight attendants or servers, who treats people as if they are beneath them. I seek out friends and employees who treat everyone with the same respect. Some people think it's a problem to be too nice, but I disagree. In fact, if I hear any manager at our company is being egotistical or political, I do my best to crush the behavior immediately.

My number one rule when I started the site—one that our editorial team still lives by today—is to never say anything about celebrities you wouldn't say to their faces. That's also a rule I follow in life: Never say something about someone you wouldn't want them to overhear if they unexpectedly appeared from around a corner. That doesn't mean I'm dishonest. I believe it's far nicer to be honest, even if telling the truth isn't easy.

After having some pretty tough bosses in past jobs in San Francisco, I knew early on that I wanted to be the type of leader who was encouraging and not intimidating. Even now, if I ever hear someone who works at POPSUGAR is scared of me, I need to figure out why, and how I can change that—it usually starts with finding common ground about something we both like so they become comfortable. There is simply no reason not to be nice or easy to talk to, whether you're the most junior employee or the boss. You don't have to be scary to be successful.

My "no mean girls" philosophy extends to our office culture. I want to create a safe, positive environment where I'd rather hear what the twenty-two-year-olds have to say than make them cower in fear. Being the new kid or the youngest employee shouldn't mean you have to do all the dirty work. At POPSUGAR, we have the mentality that everyone should know how to do a little bit of everything. Sure, you need to start by learning the basics and train your way up to bigger tasks, but being at the top doesn't mean you are ever above doing a little dirty work. That's part of working hard and playing nice and being a team player.

Being a mom to three daughters has made me even more devoted to the "play nice" philosophy. After all, I don't want them to grow up to be the mean girls. Now more than ever, I preach the nice, because I want to make sure that my girls understand that being nice is a life priority. Every day, I focus on reinforcing three important rules: Be a good sister (basically don't fight!), be a good helper (clean up your toys, bring your plates to the sink, feed the dog), and just be good (be sweet to your friends, say "please" and "thank you," don't make me repeat things twelve times). We even have a system at home to incentivize the girls to behave and do chores. Instead of allowance, we have a "gem jar," where the girls have three chances a day to get rewarded "gems" for being good. It's a little like giving out gold star stickers— which BTW, we did in the early years at POPSUGAR, and it worked on twenty-two-year-olds just as well. My daughters know their number one priority is being nice, to one another and to others. It's worked like a gem. :)

From the day we moved into our first office in mid-July 2006, right after Katie was born, I was determined to create a positive, friendly work environment. It probably helped that these early employees saw me at my most tired moments with an eight-week-old baby. They saw my passion for the company and my family. At first, I worried that the young twentysomethings working with me would not want a baby around, but Katie ended up being like our company mascot. We would take "Katie breaks" and cheer her on as she crawled for the first time or as she embarked on her many attempts to walk.

Having companions in the office (we used to let people bring their dogs, too) helped create a more loving, familiar environment. We celebrated small and big milestones often. We had lots of happy hours. We hosted dinners and award-show "working parties" at our house. Our original editorial meeting was just ten of us, literally sitting on the floor in a circle, celebrating wins and sharing ideas. It felt like summer camp—not coincidentally, one of the things I miss most about my childhood—and it was incredibly positive and encouraging.

I used to be pretty anti cheerleader until I met my favorite one, Krista, who is also one of the sweetest, smartest women I know. From the beginning, she made sure we recognized our employees for their accomplishments while rallying them to feel the fact that we're all working toward the same finish line. Even though we have five hundred employees now, I'd like to think that vibe remains the same. Brian and I loved the intimate feeling we had when we first started the company, when we had Katie running down the halls, and holiday parties with employees' spouses doing karaoke. It's sad to reach the point of growth at a company when you don't know everyone's name! But we realize if we want to be a successful, long-lasting business, we need to think beyond big while still remaining true to the "work hard, play nice" mentality. Even with our editors spread out over five cities, we still have weekly edit meetings where we gather around to hear highlights from the team. We also host company-wide social events like bar crawls, sports teams, and hackathons, where the engineers go off-site to build stuff and work crazy hours but also get to take breaks by the pool and play games at night. And Krista keeps cheer-leading, now with a weekly e-mail that spotlights standout employees nominated by their managers and peers.

As our staff of ten began to expand, Krista knew we had to get out of my head and figure out how we wanted to train the growing list of new hires. As we recruited an amazing team of people, we took note of our shared beliefs and wrote them down. At the same time, we had to continue to foster our friendly, fun, safe space online. We hired a community manager very early on to monitor comments; we wanted all the negative naysayers in the comments section to go else-where. If our readers were bold enough to upload photos of themselves in their outfits of the day—this was before #OOTD was a thing—we wanted to encourage them and get more from them. Anyone who left a comment calling people fat, ugly, or stupid quickly learned that this was not the place to share their thoughts. We took pride in creating a space to champion one another and share the love.

The company continued to grow, doors opened, and Brian and I were introduced to wonderful, very experienced peo-ple: prospective employees, board members, and business partners. We met with one woman who was very sweet to us but who gave off a very cold demeanor. Your typical ruthless, high-powered New York media executive: Think *The Devil Wears Prada*. She had a desire to take over the world, but in an extremely intimidating way. I was excited to be at the same table with her, but at the same time, I felt nauseated and uncomfortable, as if I didn't belong. I guess being away from New York might have softened my East Coast roots, though I still had the work ethic of a New Yorker—with a softer outlook on life and teamwork.

I credit my work ethic mostly to my dad's influence. I am definitely a daddy's girl, and his constant love and his encouragement to be whoever and whatever I wanted was crucial to my development. He always taught me to work hard, whether it was at school, on the soccer field, or at any job. I'm thankful my father made me work each summer in high school and during my college years, whether as a messenger at a law firm or as a sales associate who spent all day folding Levi's at Urban Outfitters. Brian lived in New York City at the time, and if I wanted to visit every weekend, I was paying my own way. I would take a super-cheap flight (only $50 if you were under twenty-five! Writing this makes me feel like my grandpa, who would tell me how he bought gum for five cents, but seriously, that price was a big deal, and, man, I wish travel was what it used to be . . . but I digress), or a four-hour train ride to go visit him almost every weekend. And as soon as I graduated from college, my dad took his credit cards away, and I was on my own.

All those years, whether I was cleaning sweat off gym

equipment or trying to figure out Excel, I always showed up early and never left until I felt I was dismissed. Playing soccer for fifteen years, I learned the importance of being there for my team. I couldn't skip practice or half-ass any games. I couldn't let my team down by not working as hard as I could, and I applied that same philosophy to my earliest jobs. I checked in with my bosses to make sure they always had what they needed from me and to find out what else I could do to help. Doing this was an important part of figuring out what I liked and what drove me to succeed, because as soon as I was at a job where I didn't want to work hard, I knew I had to make a change.

Easier said than done, I know. But I truly believe that work needs to be addictive, and that working hard is infectious. As I've said before, when I started writing for POP-SUGAR, I became addicted. So much so that when I was lucky enough to accompany Brian on business trips to Paris, I would sit in the hotel room and write nonstop. I had to force myself off the computer to take breaks to walk the glorious streets and remind myself that, as much as I loved what I was doing, I also needed to take advantage of being in such a beautiful city (that said, this was also before there was wireless in every café).

Another symptom of my addiction: I went to a BFF's bachelorette weekend in South Beach. While my friends were asleep, I sat on the bathroom floor of our hotel room to pull out the best quotes from a *Vanity Fair* article, because I knew my audience would love it. Plus, I got the earliest copies of new issues, thanks to my job in advertising, and wanted to get the story online even before *Vanity Fair* did. So there I was, on the bathroom floor, typing away, perfectly content.

Fast-forward to a year later: As I worked my ass off with a brand-new baby, the new hires who joined the company also worked harder than they had at their last jobs. We were young, fun, and working and playing hard together. That contagious energy meant we were always on and thinking of new things we wanted to launch, write, and build. Our minds were running wild in a good way: We learned from one another and shared our successes and cheered one another on when we scored.

HOW TO MAKE WORKING HARD FUN

Hard work needs to be something that drives you and makes you feel more complete. If it's not, then figure out what is holding you back and try to change it. If you love where you work, but there is something you can't stand doing, speak up and try to change it. I often ask our employees, "What is your least favorite task?" so we can figure out a way to automate the task and allow us to focus on more important things. We ask the people who are just starting, or who might be feeling burned out, to write their own description of the job they want to have. It's made us realize what roles we needed to fill and that we already had people on our team who wanted to fill them.

Having a job that's "fun" isn't the be-all and end-all. You also have to work hard, which means volunteering for extra work—even if you're just folding jeans. When I felt bored at Urban Outfitters, I volunteered to work "mark-down night," which meant weeding through racks and racks of clothes marking literally every item. It was a task the managers found tedious, but I just wanted something different. Plus, it taught me the ins and outs of the compa-ny's inventory system, which I figured might come in handy. Working hard and showing initiative will be more rewarding in the long run. You will get the good reference for your résumé, the promotion and the raise, the extra time off, and the praise and the respect. So volunteer for extra work or offer to work a weekend.

If working hard feels painful and you know it is time to make a change, at least you'll know what you don't want at your next job. In the meantime, try to identify even the little things that bring you satisfaction and use that to start shaping the vision for what could become your dream job. The goal is to make working hard fun.

THE LITTLE THINGS

- **SMILE MORE.** Hard work actually brings a smile to my face, so I figure the more I smile at people in the office, the more that feeling will be contagious. I also want everyone at POPSUGAR to know that I appreciate their hard work, and I believe a smile is a simple way to show that appreciation. I smile at people in the hallways, on the street, at the grocery store, wherever. If someone is giving a presentation, I make sure that when they make eye contact with me, I'm smiling. What can it possibly hurt to encourage the people working with me to take risks, to look out into the room and know I'm supporting them? Smiling is easy and it's infectious. You have no idea what the people next to you are going through, and sometimes a simple smile can change someone's entire mood and day. Smiling gets a bad rap because it causes wrinkles or because it's so antifeminist when we only tell women to do it. But really: It's cheap, easy, and has a positive effect on others, so I am all for it.

- **CREATE YOUR OWN SPEAK.** I've also learned to strike a balance between working quickly and still taking the time for niceties. Although I get thousands of e-mails every day, I try to respond immediately to anyone who needs me. That means I reply fast and don't deal with punctuation or capitalization (beyond what my AutoText does for me). If my book editor had seen how fast and unpunctuated my e-mails are, she probably never would have given me a book deal. Also, I'm a terrible speller. In fact, my first hire was a copy editor, because I felt that POPSUGAR needed to be seen as a legitimate news source that didn't have copy or factual errors. That said, I did make clear that I wanted my excited personality to come through in my writing, so my exclamation marks had to stay!!!

I still overuse exclamations in e-mails (maybe the only punctuation I use) and often end sentences with smiley :) and winky ;) faces to make sure my intentions come across. I started doing this well before emojis were an option—plus, emoticons work from any keyboard. The team knows it's my thing, and I love it when I see other people start to speak in emoticons. I have my own shorthand language and my own way of giving feedback to my team, but it works. I'm not suggesting that my style works for everyone. It's not suited for more formal company cultures, and probably not when you're e-mailing people outside the company. But I do think you can find your own style of e-mail that shows your personality while also being efficient.

- **SIMPLE MANNERS GO A LONG WAY.** I always make sure to say "please" and "thank you." I think manners are essential for the "work hard, play nice" mentality. This goes back to the simple rule of treating others how you want to be treated.

- **HAVE TREATS AT YOUR DESK.** Keep some treats at your desk, whatever your treat of choice may be. It could be candy, which is yummy, cheap, and easy, or it could be dried fruit, nuts, or something else healthy. Whatever it is, it will encourage people to get up from their desks and stop by and say hi.

- **MOVE IT!** The simple act of walking around can do wonders. If you sit all day, you get tired and start to drag, and others can see the dreadful stare-at-the-screen, dead-in-the-eyes look. You don't have to leave the office if you are too busy, but make sure to get up and pee, get a snack, go say hi to someone, fill up your water bottle, whatever gets your blood flowing. It's great for your brain.

- **GIVE YOURSELF GOLD STARS!** One simple thing that makes working hard more fun is looking back on your accomplishments. Don't wait for your manager to applaud your strengths in your annual performance review. Instead, allow yourself to be proud of your wins, big and small. Keep track of them and celebrate them!

9 TO 5 MORE LIKE WHENEVER TO WHENEVER THE JOB GETS DONE

I've been pregnant for what feels like half the time I've been at POPSUGAR. While I worked up until the arrival of each baby and never took maternity leave—instead, I worked from home afterward for a month—I strongly encourage everyone else to take as much leave as they feel they need. And when I was pregnant, I was happy to sit with my feet up, walk around with no shoes on, or move to community work areas like the kitchen and couch.

As the company continued to grow, so did my family. Three girls is a lot to juggle, but I feel as passionate about being home for them as I do about growing our company. I have learned to blend my daily to-dos and create a schedule that allows me to leave to coach soccer and be home for dinners and bedtime. But that doesn't mean my day ends when I leave the office. I'm taking calls or answering e-mails on the go, and I encourage my employees to do the same. I'm also back online after my kids are asleep.

We've been able to create an environment where we trust people to get their work done even if it means working at untraditional times. I tell my editors: As long as no one is waiting on you to move forward with something, then it's totally OK to sneak out to a gym class or clear your head with a trip to get some frozen yogurt. I'd much rather they leave at five to go to the gym, and answer e-mails later, than toil away at their desks until eight. Small breaks can only do so much; working out will get your endorphins up and make you happier and healthier in the long run.

If you are happy in your job and working hard at it, don't be afraid to ask for what you need, especially those small changes that can go a long way. If you have ideas on how to boost morale at the company, share them with the higher-ups. You'd be surprised how much your managers want to keep you happy if they value you and your talents. I always encourage people to speak up if there is a simple change that can make their lives easier: adjusting their schedule, sending them home early if they are working an award show that weekend, or providing breakfast once a week to everyone at the office.

CREATING A COMPANY CULTURE THAT ROCKS

In my current position, the biggest responsibility isn't just to make my work fun—it's to make it easy for everyone else to work hard and play nice, too. We've had open seating in the POPSUGAR office since day one. Neither Brian nor I has ever had an office. In fact, the only "office" we did have, in the first years, was a room for Katie to nap and play. When I travel to our other offices, I sit wherever there is an open desk. I don't care if it's next to reception, the interns, or my direct reports. I sit wherever is easiest, and I'm not picky about it. I want people to hear me talk about last night's *Scandal* or *GOT*. Being part of what used to be called watercooler talk is a way to break down the scary and have everyone feel on the same level.

I still make an effort to get to know all of our new hires. Obviously, as I've gotten older and as our company has grown, I can't be at every happy hour. But I want this job to be fun and playful for the new hires. I make an effort to ensure the socializing is still happening, and often I invite the team over to my house, where we work together in real time and watch live events like the Emmys. It reminds everyone that this is how and why the fun started; when ten of us are in the room together, the creativity reaches a whole new level, and a glass of wine as the night goes on makes the endless hours more enjoyable.

People are more likely to work hard when they feel comfortable, when it's a friendly, honest, and authentic environment. Even though honesty can be tough to deal with, I truly believe that people appreciate authenticity. Being authentic doesn't mean you should have zero filter, but you also shouldn't sugarcoat things. Letting your personality come through—even if your work persona isn't exactly like the "you" of your personal life—builds trust and fosters communication. If you're funny, be funny; if you're sincere, be sincere. If you cry at commercials or count Justin Bieber among your guilty pleasures, it's OK to admit it. If your team can see you being a real person, they'll feel more comfortable being honest with you, too.

Just as all of our editors know our number one rule (don't say anything about a celebrity that you wouldn't say to their face), we also train our managers to provide lots of specific feedback to employees, both positive and negative, which builds trust with our teams and keeps people engaged at work. Of course, there's nothing wrong at all with paying an impromptu compliment, but you also need to go beyond saying "nice work" or "thank you" when someone is basically just doing her job. It's much more meaningful to recognize specific accomplishments and explain why they are good; it shows you are paying attention and serves a useful purpose.

Same goes for negative feedback: If you keep it constructive and provide context that explains why it's being addressed, the feedback doesn't come off as scolding. Make sure the employee understands the feedback and why it's important. Of course, delivering negative feedback is never easy, but being honest is an essential part of playing nice. If someone is doing something wrong, especially when it could hurt their career or their reputation, it's crucial that you say something. Otherwise, it's just not fair.

Don't wait for the annual review to deliver critical feedback either. Bring up issues as early and often as possible so the person has time to correct them; otherwise you're just setting him up to fail. It sounds overly simple, but think about what you would want to hear if it were you, and use that to govern when and how you deliver feedback. We also encourage feedback as a two-way conversation. As managers, we encourage our teams to tell us what they need more or less of from us and to share what's making them happy or unhappy. As long as you are honest and direct, you should absolutely offer feedback to your boss, too, and if you're not getting enough from her, ask for more. We want to know if there is an obstacle preventing you from making hard work fun, and we can't fix a problem unless we know it's there.

Let's do a speed round right now. Think about the last month at your job, or even the last year, and answer these questions.

- When did working hard feel addictive?

- How did you make working hard more fun, for yourself or someone else?

- When did you feel most appreciated and most unappreciated?

- What's your favorite thing and least favorite thing about your day-to-day tasks?

- What more do you wish you were getting from your manager?

- Are you one of the first ones in the office and/or last to leave?

- Are you someone who looks at the clock often at work or loses track of time?

- Do you speak up in meetings or make suggestions to your coworkers via e-mail?

- Do you continue to stay available via phone, e-mail, etc., after hours by choice?

- Do you offer advice to coworkers and help take tasks off others' to-do lists?

CHAPTER 5

MAJOR IN YOUR HEALTH

I'm a sugar addict of the worst kind. One reason I was so happy to marry Brian (aside from the fact that he's awesome) was that the last name Sugar was so perfect for me. Seriously, the amount of sugar I eat is not good for anyone. I sneak candy throughout the day and even stop halfway through my salad at lunchtime to eat chocolate. When our team is working hard on award-show nights, I bring the treats. I even have a special stash of candy just for writing this book, which is nicer than my everyday candy, so it's a rare treat that keeps me motivated. (Special thanks to Sugarfina's rainbow Kyoto Blossom candies for their help as I write all these chapters.)

Looking back on my life, this shouldn't come as a shock.

Recently, I was digging up old photos to use as #TBT pics on Instagram, and I found dozens of photos of my two-year-old self drinking cans of Coke. I was shocked. I would never give that to my kids. Also, I went to bed only after having dessert pretty much every night. My forty-four-year-old brother still has a glass of milk and cookies before bed.

I don't blame my parents, though. Back then, it was the norm to give kids soda, and my parents were fun and laid-back. We were a fairly healthy household, but we all have a sweet tooth. The same way we all have bad knees—it's genetic and was probably bound to happen anyway. :) While I won't be giving my kids Coke anytime soon, I don't want to deny them the joy of dessert that I grew up with. In our house, it's a few jelly beans or one marshmallow per night. Definitely no chocolate, which is mostly selfish because it's impossible to get them in bed after that. Oh, and the waffles with ice cream that I had with my family every Sunday is allowed only on special occasions like birthdays.

BEND IT LIKE ~~BECKHAM~~ SUGAR

That said, as much as I love sweets, I have always been incredibly active. I was an active kid with athletic parents: Dad played soccer, Mom played tennis; my whole family was very athletic. I still remember going to watch my father play soccer when I was young. My neighborhood was mostly boys, and I grew up with an older brother. I would play capture the flag until sunset, when we had to go home for dinner. My parents encouraged me to try new sports, and over the years, I sampled everything from gymnastics to swim team to track. But ultimately, I fell in love with soccer, starting at age five. I spent fifteen years as a highly competitive player, and now that passion continues through my children. It's the sport that helped teach me the teamwork and leadership qualities I still use today. Playing sports made me understand that even if you are an excellent individual player, you need to surround yourself with people who have different talents in order to grow. "Playing up" challenges you to perform at a higher level and become an even better player.

Moving my body and staying active are just as important as indulging. I am constantly looking for ways to curb my sweet tooth without denying myself—because we only live once and I want to live life to the fullest. The other challenge is to stay healthy while working hard running a company and raising three girls, but I swear, it is possible. The answer is in finding solutions for healthy living that are easy, fun, and addictive, whether that means becoming obsessed with a good-for-me food or finding a workout that I can't resist.

I believe mental and physical health are different for every body and mind. No two of us are programmed to be healthy the same way. Some people learn that meditation is the key to clearing their heads. Though it's on my list of things to try, for now, my form of meditating is a nice, long shower where no one bothers me and I can think about the day ahead. I have friends who get an insane amount of satisfaction out of running marathons, but I have never enjoyed running long distances. And while I have a sweet tooth but have never been much of a drinker, I know plenty of people who would rather have a glass of wine than a cookie any day.

How we choose to stay healthy can also change over time; you might find that an exercise that used to make you feel great changes as you age and as your lifestyle changes. That's why it's important to keep trying new things, and the earlier you can commit to taking care of yourself, the better.

I know, I know, exercise, moderate drinking, and nutrition might be the last thing on your mind when you're in your twenties, having a blast, dating like crazy, and trying to get your career off the ground. But if you start establishing healthy habits in your twenties, you'll find it easier to stick to them as you get older. In your thirties and forties, especially if you have kids, it only gets harder to maintain a healthy weight, find time to exercise, and get plenty of sleep. Those hangovers feel way worse, too—at least that's what I can tell from observing the drinking routines of Brian and my other friends over the years.

EATING HEALTHY WITHOUT BEING MISERABLE

Despite my lifelong consumption of sugar, I did establish some healthy habits in my youth, and for that I'm incredibly grateful. As a kid, I never left home without eating breakfast. I always needed something to kick-start my day, whether it was cereal, a bagel, or eggs. Living on my own in college and into my adult life, I always made a continued effort to eat breakfast. I'm still a big believer in starting your day by fueling your body, though now I change it up with healthier options (probably the West Coast influence) like kale-pineapple smoothies, overnight oats with chia seeds, or egg and turkey sausage muffins—not the McMuffin kind, though after our annual office parties, we tend to indulge in hash browns and McMuffins all around.

Purely by chance, I always preferred healthier versions of certain foods, often without even knowing they were healthier. For example, I really dislike egg yolks; I have always preferred egg whites, way before they were declared the healthier thing to do . . . though now everything is all pro-yolk again, but whites are still lower in calories. Who can keep it all straight? I also dislike sour cream, mayonnaise, and other (mostly unhealthy) condiments. Brian is the opposite: He likes to load up on spicy sauces and calls what I eat "bland, boring food." But really, I just like to taste whatever it is I am eating without all the extras: meat with no steak sauce, turkey with no mayo. (The exception is French fries, which always taste better with ketchup.) I also love avocados, which have that good fat. ;)

I also LOVE lemons. Like, as a kid, I ate lemons straight up to the point that my dentist told me to stop because it was taking the enamel off my teeth. Turns out, lemons are all sorts of good for you; they help digestion and deliver lots of vitamin C. I've been doing this natural detox my whole life without even knowing it. However, for the sake of my teeth, I did ditch the raw lemon slices in favor of lemon water, which I drink every night before bed and throughout the day.

Still, I'm not here to tell you that you have to drink five gallons of lemon water a day. Even I wish I drank more water! We always hear that healthy people drink so much water or green tea, and of course it's important to stay hydrated. But if you don't like green tea or lemon water, don't feel obligated to choke it down. I think everyone should find their own (healthy) liquid of choice. For me it's Vitaminwater or something with lemons!

You could spend all day reading advice about healthy eating (I highly recommend POPSUGAR Fitness) and what to eat to lose weight, beat bloat, boost your metabolism, and get the nutrition you need. But unless you are some sort of superhero, it's impossible to follow every rule, and I think life is too short for that anyway. It's important to educate yourself about nutrition so that you don't make unhealthy choices when you think you're making healthy ones. But once you understand the basics of healthy eating, you should figure out what makes the most sense for you, and that may change over time.

Our Fitness editors would tell you to bring a healthy lunch from home every day, but that's just not realistic for me. My mornings are focused on kids, and my work days are fast-paced, so it's easier just to order. To make sure I get my veggies, I have a salad almost every day, but it has to have lots of goodies. Luckily, I tend toward healthy goodies. I love a salad with grilled chicken and parmesan cheese, but instead of a classic Caesar dressing, I prefer citrus vinaigrette or oil and lemon. I love cheese, but I'll also add fruit (strawberries, mango, dried cranberries), pumpkin seeds, edamame, and hearts of palm. Soup is another favorite, and a way to get more liquids.

Another piece of advice you always hear is to cook dinner at home rather than eat out. But everyone knows that cooking every single night just isn't realistic when you have a job, or kids, or both. At my house, we tend to cook dinner three or four nights a week (usually chicken, meat, or pasta) and order in a couple of nights as well. We are a huge pasta and pizza family, which is the Italian side of me that I will never get away from, so I compromise by making breakfast and lunch healthier. Brian also loves to cook, especially big Sunday dinners, and our daughter Juliet happens to love it, too, so she often gets in on the action. We've gotten lucky with some great sitters who love to cook, and dinner involves a lot of teamwork: Our caretaker, Cary, might pick up food and start prepping so Brian or I can whip it up soon after we walk through the door.

Like mental and physical health, eating well is different for different people. You know better than anyone what you really want to indulge in and what you'll happily sacrifice. The key is finding a balance and trying not to obsess about it. Even though I try to eat healthy, I don't want my mental health to suffer either, so I don't beat myself up about ordering takeout or using other shortcuts that make my life easier, like buying a premade meal at Whole Foods or Postmating dinner.

My biggest downfall is snacks. Since I really do crave sweets constantly, I try to opt for an orange or chocolate-covered almonds, but I don't deny myself salty popcorn or pretzels if it's what I really want. Snacks are a double-edged sword, because I don't want to oversnack, but I don't want to get cranky, either. Like many people, I experience low blood sugar if I don't get a snack when I need it, and I get irritated very quickly. My dad always reminded me to carry snacks, because he didn't want to deal when I got bitchy (and I don't blame him). Being a mom has reinforced this snacking habit more. I've learned to recognize when I am in a bad mood because I just need to eat something; though it's clear when you work in an office that not everyone has figured that out. I always keep a few fruit bars that I enjoy stashed in my purse, and if I have my favorite edamame, pumpkin seed, and dried berry snack on hand, I'm less likely to reach for candy . . . again.

Try to find a healthy snack that you can get addicted to, and don't assume that because a recipe is good for you that it won't be good. You never know when you're going to find a healthy food you're obsessed with. I promise, it is possible. It even works with my kids. Yes, we have our Goldfish cravings, but every weekend is full of carrots, cucumbers, and hummus. As much as I am NOT gluten-free, I have been convinced to try a few recipes that have become huge hits at my house. The latest is a banana, egg, and almond butter pancake. I cannot cook them fast enough. I also like to experiment with new grains: Currently, farro is my BFF, but I also like couscous and quinoa. That said, I don't shy away from Uncle Ben's rice, either, and though my daughters love fruit, we also have fruit gummies at the house. I don't give my kids Coke like my parents did, but I don't deny them healthier sodas or a sip of soda (preferably a cleaner kind) here and there either. I think it's totally OK (and more realistic) to enjoy both super-healthy and not-so-healthy foods as long as you keep a healthy balance.

BODY BEFORE AND AFTER BABY

Growing up as an athlete has its advantages and disadvantages. On the one hand, I have always been in good shape and I'm used to getting my body moving on a regular basis. On the other hand, the idea of exercising just for exercise's sake can be hard to get used to. Throughout my life, I've had several defining moments involving exercise, when the way I work out changed in dramatic ways. But in each phase of my life, I have found something that works for me.

When I went to college, it was the first time I wasn't on a team, where I had scheduled practices or an established workout routine. It was hard to find a way to motivate myself my first year, so I made sure to walk a lot, at the very least. But by sophomore year, I felt that walking wasn't enough, so I joined a gym. It was weird to be working out alone, with no game to prep for and no set schedule to build a routine around. I had to do a morning here and an afternoon there based on my class schedule. But because it was important to me to stay active, I made it work.

Eventually, I became very comfortable in a gym. At my jobs after college, we got discounted gym memberships as perks, and I made sure to use them. I was pretty consistent in making time a few days a week to spend an hour at the gym: elliptical, stretching, weights, the usual. I encourage anyone who gets gym perks at their job to take advantage of them. Even if you have never been a gym person, you can use it as a place to experiment and find the exercise that feels good to you. You will never know if you love yoga or running or Zumba or Pilates unless you try it, and sometimes just taking a class with a good instructor can make you love something you used to hate.

I loved having physical therapy after my knee surgery, because it felt like I had a personal trainer. I had to keep working out to keep my knee strong—plus, I was almost thirty. I knew metabolism changes were coming and I wanted to spend my thirties having babies, so I was prepared to try harder to feel good about my body. When I was working from home after just starting POPSUGAR, it was the first time I had to force myself to get off-line for an hour every day and go work out, partly because of my knee but also because if I didn't force myself to take breaks, I would be hunched over my laptop in my pj's all day. I would walk my doggies in the morning and at night and aim to break for lunch and the gym in the early afternoon.

When I was pregnant with my first daughter, I got even more into working out because I wanted to prepare myself for extreme circumstances. I had just had knee surgery, and I had no idea how big I was going to get or how hard it would be to lose the weight. Everything I had read said to just keep working out as long as you can. I didn't overextend myself, but I wanted to feel strong and not gross after my pregnancy. I carved out four days a week for a solid forty-five- to sixty-minute workout—usually thirty minutes on the elliptical, ten minutes of stretching, and twenty minutes doing a weight circuit—mostly to keep my legs strong.

Most of the time I felt awesome afterward, but as I got larger, it definitely got harder to feel energized after a workout versus just feeling really tired.

Exercise might seem like the easiest thing to let go when life gets crazy, but not taking a break to move around can actually make things feel worse. If you find yourself feeling tired or stressed or always hurting, your body is probably trying to tell you something. Once Katie was born and we were working like crazy building the company, I didn't have any free time to spare. But I found myself wanting a break every day at 4:00 P.M., so I knew I still needed to find time to clear my head and feel strong. Most afternoons, I would head to the gym with Krista. Going at that time let us beat the crowd, and we'd even have short meetings on the way over and back to the office.

FITTING IN FITNESS

It really helps to dedicate a time of day or certain days every week when you know you're going to work out. Treat it like anything else you would schedule in your calendar. At the beginning of every week, map out your gym days alongside meetings and happy hours, and do your best to stick to it. But if you just can't one day and you need to skip the gym, don't beat yourself up about it as long as you keep up that long-term commitment. I like SoulCycle because it forces me to sign up for classes every Monday at noon, so that when they flip the switch and hundreds of people are trying to get into the same class, my spot is secured. Having the same few classes to go to each week helps me stay in a routine. That said, there are days when I don't get in or I have to skip class for one of my kids' soccer games, and I remind myself that it's OK. I have a lifetime commitment to fitness, and if I have to miss one class, I know I will find another way to move my body.

As my job evolved and my family grew, my workouts changed, too. After my second daughter, I did feel gross, and losing the weight was difficult. I'm fortunate to not have struggled with body issues, but this was the first time in my life that I didn't feel like myself. I wasn't the type to try trendy fitness classes, but I needed something different. I started taking barre classes, since all the women in my office were raving about it. At first, I felt super uncomfortable because it was out of my comfort zone to leave the familiar gym world, and I was weak compared to the others in the class. But it worked, and I got strong! After a few months, I noticed real changes in my body. I felt more comfortable about my body at thirty-three than I ever had before. Then I got pregnant again. ;)

With three kids, my routine changed yet again. This was when my love of SoulCycle started. I joke that the first rule of SoulCycle is that you talk only about SoulCycle. I look forward to my weekend classes like no other workout I've had before. It's like my combined therapy and exercise. I realize it is a luxury to be able to afford expensive classes, but I am also investing in my health, because for me, exercise is a must. I feel gross and even depressed if I go a few days without some sort of movement. After class, I come home feeling clearheaded, stronger, and happier. My husband encourages my weekend ritual and watches our kids so I can enjoy it fully. If I can't get to SoulCycle, my exercise might be a dance party in my house with the kids, but I need to do *something*.

Through all of my exercise phases, one thing that has stayed constant is my love of long walks. I have always cherished walks, whether exploring (or getting lost in) an unfamiliar city like Paris or spending Sunday in New York with Brian walking our dog from our apartment downtown to Central Park. During the week, walking in New York was a sport, and I could win it every day. I loved the hustle of the city (though maybe not the smells), the people-watching, and the fact that I could change up my route constantly. In San Francisco, the hills make walking more challenging, but the views are so killer it's worth it. Whether I'm walking my dogs, my kids, or myself, I've learned that being outside is crucial to my happiness. I'm lucky that San Francisco has so much natural light, because if I still lived in NYC, I'd need to do some sort of light therapy. Seasonal affective disorder is a real thing. When it's super cold in winter and we can't go outside, it just does weird things to our biology.

I get cabin fever very easily, and it got worse when I moved to San Francisco, where the seasons aren't well defined and almost every day feels like a perfect fall day on the East Coast. In New York, it was easier to hibernate in the winter and spend as much time as possible outside the rest of the year. But in San Francisco, no matter what the season, the sun can be shining, the dogs have to go out, and the kids need to play, and so I go out, too.

Nowadays, besides wanting to be outside and smell the fresh air, I use walks to take care of things I need to do. I walk to work as many days a week as I can—it's about two miles door to door. Brian and I also walk our kids to school, and once we've dropped them off, we walk to work together and use the time to make family plans or talk about work. If I'm alone, I make phone calls to my team on the East Coast or to my parents. I can even tackle e-mails as I walk, but never when I cross the street!

When you work all day in an office, nothing beats getting outside. We spend a lot of time at our desks. Over the years, we've found all kinds of ways to make them more comfortable, like better chairs, balance-ball seats, and now standing desks. All these advancements are great, but they can't match getting your body moving.

My calendar is usually packed, but I try to block off an

hour from twelve to one every day to catch up on e-mail or just provide a cushion in case of any fire drills. But if it's a fairly normal day, that hour break forces me to get up and get outside, hopefully, walking with some coworkers and getting to catch up while we grab lunch. Some days I use it to knock out some talking points, but most of the time, I just use that time to chat casually to the team, break from whatever we are heads-down on and clear our minds. On hot days, we take fro-yo breaks. Even if it's only a quick ten-minute food run, I come back to my desk with my blood flowing and my head clear and ready to dive back in.

HAPPY DAYS

Feeling young, wild, and free in Hawaii at age seven. This was the
beginning of my love affair with the tropical islands. I had found my
happy place. I knew I had to get back someday.

Maui, 1982

THE WONDER YEARS

Growing up outside DC with my cute outfits (thanks to my mom)
and the curly hair I was about to lose control of.

Grimaldi Family, 1980

HEROES

This Daddy's Little Girl
always had a great role
model to look up to. I
often called him my hero
and my driving force to
live my happiest life.

*My Bat Mitzvah,
November 11, 1989*

FAMILY TIES

Cousin time was always special for me.
It still is—even if I'm not the baby anymore. :)

1981

THE A-TEAM

Soccer began to play a major role
in my life. Winning and working
hard (with a smile) became an
early obsession.

1986

FRIENDS

My oldest friend, Lisa, and
I were born ten days apart.
Our friendship is one of a
kind. #bighairdontcare

1989

HOW I MET YOUR MOTHER

Brian joins us on our family trip to Hawaii. We are literally glowing in what is now our shared happy place.

Kauai, 1997

CLUELESS

School's out forever, and I'm off to New York City to be with Brian and start my next chapter—whatever that was going to be.

George Washington University Graduation, 1998

CHEERS

Party on! I spent my twenties cheering on friends as they got engaged, showered, and married.

My Bachelorette Party, 1999

ONCE UPON A TIME

The fairy tale officially begins.

September 25, 1999

CALIFORNICATION

My early 2000s were spent taking care of these two pups in the city by the Bay.

Lucy and Jack, 2004

MY SO-CALLED LIFE

Mixing work with play at a fun POPSUGAR event.

2012

MARRIED . . . WITH CHILDREN

Back to "work" just days after Katie was born.

June 2006

THE OFFICE

Katie working hard at the POPSUGAR offices.

2008

MODERN FAMILY

POPSUGAR was growing really fast and becoming one big family.

2011

AMERICAN IDOL

Each site featured
an illustration of
a woman who
embodied the
various personalities
of our staff and our
readers. This one
was POPSUGAR.

2007

2014

THE GOLDEN GIRLS

From starting
POPSUGAR with one
of my best friends
to curating Must
Have Boxes with
the edit team, every
day and night is an
adventure. . . .

2016

ENTOURAGE

Nothing beats the swim, sun, and sand with my family.
We love our happy place.

Kona, 2016

Questionnaire: Are you majoring in your health?

- What do you do to start your morning off right?

- What do you consider your healthiest habit?

- What do you consider your least healthy habit?

- What type of exercise do you really love?

- How do you make time to feel good physically?

- How do you clear your head during the day?

- What little things make you happiest during the week?

CHAPTER 6

MOVING PAST THE CRAPPY STUFF

Shit happens—to everyone! You don't deserve special treatment because you are having a bad day. People face death, being dumped, ridiculous Uber surge pricing, and bad hair days all the time. It's how you grow from these catastrophes, big and small, that shape you into who you become.

And by the way, it only gets worse the older you get. In the past two years I've seen more death, illnesses, divorce, affairs, and straight-up bullshit than I'd like to recall. So far, I have been extremely fortunate to not experience anything super traumatic directly; however, I've been close enough to it to feel it. I am incredibly sympathetic when my friends are in pain and will do anything I can to help ease it. I'm there for them when they need me during tough times. In fact, seeing this has been great therapy. The bad stuff makes me take notice of the small and big things in my life that are easy to miss as time flies by. As I try to be here for my friends in need, in a weird, terrible way it's very therapeutic because I see close up how bad it can be. It stops me in my tracks to make sure I am appreciating all I have.

We all have days when we can't get out of a funk, when we just want to wallow in it, when it seems like nothing is going our way, or when everything seems out of our control. When that happens, I try to keep perspective and ask myself, is it really that bad? I remind myself that the flip side is on the horizon and I just need to get there. Until then, I try to find a happy place beyond whatever is bugging me, whether it's closing my eyes and dreaming of a warm beach, getting ice cream with my kids, or getting on that bike at SoulCycle.

URGH: LET IT GO

I am an optimist, but I get tired, cranky, mad, and sad just like anyone else. It's hard to manage one hundred people creating content and never get angry. Although we provide our editors with very intense training, some new hires can take a little longer to get the voice and vision. While it's very rare, I've definitely had moments when I looked at the site and thought "WTF?! How did this story get posted? Is anyone even reading this besides me?" In some cases, I learn I need to let it go and allow the editors to push my boundaries about what we cover and what we don't. Sometimes, I will reach out to the person who edited the piece (sheltering the new hire from my harsh feedback!) and give feedback on how or why this should be edited.

Other times, my anger is outward-facing: Our "be nice" attitude often means we don't get the credit we deserve for being the first to discover a trend or for getting a great quote that's going viral but that no one is attributing to us. But I've learned to let go of that stuff—and trust karma to take over.

GET ANGRY

Playing nice doesn't mean I never get angry, frustrated, upset, or flat-out pissed off. As much as I try to stay balanced, sometimes I just need to vent. The key is learning how to get angry the right way.

It's important to know who to talk to when you are angry. And, I'm sorry to say, it's probably best if that person is not a coworker. Even if you are super close with a colleague, it's better to reach out to a supportive friend, a sibling, or even your mom (in fact, you'd probably make her day, because moms love to listen and help, no matter how old you are). Even if no one else will know exactly what you are talking about, it doesn't matter: You just need to get things off your chest. And if you turn to your friend at work, you spread that bad energy, and you'll find both of you are feeding off a bad vibe that lasts a lot longer than it needs to. That said, if you're not merely venting but are trying to find a solution, a coworker (as long as he or she is your peer) can be a great resource, but so can people who are on the outside.

I will often write nasty e-mails that I don't ever send. Actually *sending* a heated, emotional e-mail can be dangerous, but sometimes, I just need to write things out and get a good night's sleep. Then, in the clarity of morning, I'll realize a civil phone call or face-to-face conversation is far more productive. A frustrated e-mail rarely solves any problems.

Instead, I've learned it's important to share my frustrations with my team productively, so I don't see repeated mistakes or, even worse, get resentful. If it's something that doesn't need an immediate response, I take the time to process the best way to deliver the feedback. In most cases— because I explain how and why something is wrong and couple it with alternate solutions or examples—the team understands my feedback well, which saves me from getting frustrated about the same thing twice.

Writing in a journal at night has also helped me control my feelings of angst. I used to be amazing about writing in it every night. Unfortunately, after my second daughter turned one, I stopped writing as much, and I still miss it terribly. Journaling was a way for me to get out my frustration and work through things that I was upset about.

Journaling, even if it's just a few lines each day, can help you recognize patterns in the things that are making you angry. Rather than simply venting to your coworkers over IM, make a productive list of the things that annoy you, enrage you, or frustrate you at work. Also write down the things that make you feel happy and fulfilled.

GET HELP!

The idea of "having it all" gets thrown around a lot these days. I can't stand when I am asked if I have achieved this goal. Yes, I feel extremely fortunate for my family, life, and what I get to do every day, but if I have it all already, then where is the drive to continue to work hard to make POP-SUGAR even more successful, learn how to face a new parenting obstacle, or find time to binge-watch a show I have on my list? There is always more. It's not greed in this case. It's balance, and "all" is different for everyone because "all" is subjective. I feel so grateful to spend my days the way I do, but that doesn't mean I don't get stressed or can do it by myself. I need help and there are many days when I feel maxed out. The best we can do is to work hard, have good intentions, and live with no regrets. That is what "all" is to me right now. It might even change by the time this book is published.

We all need help sometimes, and you have to know when to ask for it. Starting a company with a brand-new baby, for instance, I relied heavily on a caretaker for help. When POPSUGAR moved into our first offices in July 2006 and Katie's room was the only "office" in the office, I was nursing her between meetings. While I loved loved loved having our first daughter at the office with us, it wasn't easy to juggle, especially as POPSUGAR grew.

Within a few months of founding the company, we started being courted by some wonderful venture capitalists. I was incredibly flattered. Brian had raised money for his other start-ups in the past, so he knew investment would help us grow faster. We put the finishing touches on the business plan, and he pitched partners at various firms while I held down the fort, writing content. It felt a little bit like a job interview process. Potential investors came to see our offices, and they were all super-smart people who seemed genuinely excited about what we were building. But when Michael Moritz from Sequoia Capital came in to meet the team, it immediately felt right. Not that there was anything wrong with the other investors, but just like in a job interview, when you feel compatible with someone, you should trust your instincts and go for it. Sequoia invested in POPSUGAR in September 2006.

Now we needed to launch ten more verticals, and we had the money to do it. We took in money by September and the plan was to have six sites up by the end of the year! While I was thrilled to have already hired some talented people who understood the POPSUGAR voice and vision, I had to think bigger. I quickly realized I needed people with "real" writing experience—you know, like a degree in journalism, as I mentioned earlier in the book. Someone who was a grammar geek but also cool and hip who would be excited about the content we were going to create together. This brings me to employee number eleven, Nancy Einhart. She was referred to us by Om, the same journalist who had encouraged me to start this site in the first place, so I knew I needed to meet her. Her job interview consisted of our taking Katie for a walk in her stroller during Nancy's lunch break from her job at one of those established tech magazines. Almost ten years later, she is still with us. In fact, she's helping me write this book, and I couldn't do any of this without her!

Sometimes, things just get heavy. Running a company can feel like a lot of weight on my shoulders. When this happens, I make sure to ask for help. When I still worked every weekend, that meant hiring a sitter to help with Katie. Now it's relying on team members to take on a project for me, having a colleague attend a meeting on my behalf, or working with other moms on scheduling car pools. Because as much as I want to pull my weight, I know I can't possibly make enough time to do everything that has to get done in a day. There is nothing wrong with asking for help and gathering a team at home and work to make life more manageable. In fact, it's an important part of creating your own success.

DEAL WITH THE CRAP

You will never stop encountering challenges in life. Even after creating my dream job and starting POPSUGAR, nothing was simply easy. For almost the entire first year of the company's existence, I felt sick every day. At the time, I blamed my nausea on postpregnancy hormones, but when I asked my doctor, she thought I was nuts. :) I now realize it was actually stress from the realization that so many people were dependent on us for their paychecks.

Though I'm no longer fighting for a raise or a promotion, running our business for ten years (and counting) comes with its own uncontrollable obstacles, some of which I never even knew existed. Along with the joy of hiring people comes the difficulty of knowing when it's not working out with an employee. We've made a few bets that didn't pan out and had to pull the plug on projects that weren't working, which meant having to let people go who we really liked working with. And for every new project we are excited about, we have to make tough decisions to not invest in other areas of opportunities. It's these hard choices that keep us up at night, but it's also inevitable as any company grows.

While POPSUGAR plays by the rules, we have seen plenty of sketchy companies doing things we would never condone. I've been adamant that we won't resort to the same tactics, even if only we know the truth. I believe that karma will get them in the end. More important, I know that we just need to stay the course, even if competitors are making more noise or not playing by the rules. We need to stay focused on our end goal, not someone else's.

Whatever the challenge you're facing, it's important to do the same and keep perspective on the very big picture, whether your ultimate goal is happiness or success or some combination of the two. Although obstacles can derail us for a little while, overcoming them is the only way to get back on the path toward what you want.

That's why rejection isn't the worst thing that can happen. In fact, getting rejected or getting dumped can actually be a good thing, because of what you'll learn from it. In time, you'll realize that many obstacles are actually a blessing; it's your life giving you clues. Being in a job you hate can give you a better understanding of what you want to do with your life. Breakups can teach you the difference between bad relationships and a good one, as can ending a toxic friendship. Knowing when to leave is the first step to getting what you really want. After some time away from a job or a relationship, you will often realize that you actually needed more, or that it wasn't as great as you thought it was.

Even losing a loved one can teach you something positive. I've had friends who have lost parents and gained a better understanding of the kind of parents they want to be. In high school, I went to several funerals of those too young to die. Seeing someone young and healthy leave the world unexpectedly is so shocking and scary, but the experience reminded me to live each day to the fullest.

I'm grateful to have friends who feel like family, but seeing my friends lose loved ones has taught me how painful and life-changing loss can be. So painful I can't even imagine. I mean, the death of my first dog, Jack, in 2012, felt more heart-wrenching to me than I would have ever imagined, and I know that doesn't come close to losing a family member. But I do know that when we experience loss, we become better equipped to handle the next obstacle life throws our way. As much as it sucks, the ability to deal with adversity is something we all need.

QUIT THAT SHIT

Even things that begin joyfully, like landing a job, can turn into crap. You might search for months for the perfect job and then find that it's not what you love. Many of us have been there, and if you haven't, you're lucky. You might even hate the job, which can feel like the worst thing ever.

Often, it's disappointing because we aren't given the tools we need to succeed. At the very least, when you are hired, you should get a complete job description explaining its purpose and what you're doing every day. You should talk to your manager about short- and long-term goals. Hell, at the very least, someone should show you where the bathroom is and tell you where the good lunch spots are. If you find yourself hired and it feels like a bait and switch, if it's something totally different from the job you were excited about, immediately talk to your manager or HR. But otherwise, be patient.

With the exception of a completely hostile environment, it's important to stick it out at a job for at least six months to a year. Unless you are being abused mentally or physically, you owe it to yourself and to the company to see if you can make it work. After all, you both had some attraction to each other to begin with—even if it's simply that you need to make some money. You can always learn something to take away for the next job.

Take notes on what is bothering you. Is it that you're not being appreciated? Not being set up to succeed? Not being spoken to like a human being? The range is very broad here. Once you know what it is, you can figure out your next steps. If it's something you feel confident talking to your manager about, then do it. If it's something you don't feel comfortable sharing with your manager, then trust your HR team. Just don't go spreading poison to coworkers. Not only can that bite you back, but it also makes you unhappier. Try to keep a positive attitude, no matter how stressed out or dissatisfied you are. This shows that you can handle more responsibility, a promotion, or something new.

Sometimes, you like where you work, but you desperately need a change. The good news is that companies change so much and so often these days that if you stay alert and engaged, you can spot your next opportunity. If you like where you work and they like you, speak up before you get totally fed up. If you think you deserve more credit or more money or if you feel stifled or bored, tell the higher-ups. If they value you, you might be able to change your job for the better, without having to endure a lengthy employment search. Also, don't feel you have to leave a job just because your friends are leaving. Trust your gut.

That said, if you are not learning, not happy, or not feeling challenged, then it might be time to move on. But don't quit in a moment of anger, especially if you need the paycheck. Instead, set a deadline for yourself. Scan job listings, reach out to contacts in your network, and update your résumé. Sometimes, just looking for a new job can make the old one a little more tolerable, because there is an end in sight. Every day, go home and write cover letters and apply to any jobs that look promising. Do your homework: Talk to past coworkers who left the same company and find out if they are happy or deeply regretting their move. Finding a new job takes time, and you may have to cut back on going out or on shopping (which will also help you save money). But remind yourself that this horrible job won't last forever and your social life will suffer only temporarily.

When I left my very first job at Young & Rubicam, I gave the standard two weeks' notice, which was totally OK. I was only there a year, and the team understood that by going to the client side and taking a job at Showtime, I was still in the family. When I left my second job, it was because I was moving across the country. I was only there six months, so I was sad to be leaving so soon. It was unexpected and it wasn't easy, but I wanted to leave on good terms. Even though I left around the holidays, I gave three weeks' notice, transitioned out gradually, and closed out all my projects.

The hardest was leaving my job at Goodby. I was there for more than five years, and I really loved the company and culture. But I was very over the job itself. I was tired and starting to feel unappreciated. I needed surgery on my knee and I wanted to focus on our family. When I was back up and running again, I returned as a freelancer, but eventually, I came to realize I needed a new outlet. I wanted to write, and if I couldn't write, I needed to get out of media planning and get away from Excel charts and managing budgets. I went on some interviews for branding companies, because I loved the strategy side of brand building, but didn't get any job offers, so I decided it was time to pave my own path. When I left for good to start POPSUGAR, I left on good terms, no hard feelings.

Though I've left only a handful of jobs, I've watched plenty of other people leave during my ten years running POPSUGAR, and trust me: There is a right way and a wrong way to leave a job. When you do decide to leave a job, which you most likely will at some point, it's incredibly important to leave it gracefully.

Often, people think you can't tell your boss you are unhappy and thinking of leaving without getting blacklisted or in trouble in some way. But you absolutely can! If you have been with a company for more than three years, consider talking to your managers before you accept the next offer—especially if you have moved up the ladder and been given opportunities to grow. Chances are, those three years together have been memorable and appreciation is mutual, and if you just need a change, you might find one within the company. If you don't, start planning your next steps.

Giving two weeks' notice, as I did at Y&R, is perfectly acceptable. Be considerate to your coworkers and don't include holidays or paid time off in your two weeks. You never know who you might cross paths with in the future. If you have been in your job for more than four years or manage a large team, consider giving even more notice if possible, and do whatever you can to ease your transition. This leaves your manager with a positive impression, which is important should you need her for a reference or ever decide you want to come back.

Even if you hate every single thing about your job, your manager, or your team, remain humble and respectful on your way out—and that applies to social media updates, too. Bad-mouthing can easily make its way back to your company and come back to haunt you. As much as you can, be grateful and polite, maybe even send a thank-you note to your manager if you're parting on good terms. I have rehired people who left POPSUGAR, but only when they left in the right way.

Questions to ask yourself after the not-so-fun stuff

- Why do you think it didn't work out?

- What did you do wrong or right?

- What warning signs might you have missed?

- What fears and worries do you have as a result of this obstacle?

- Who can you reach out to for support?

Things that might make you feel better, aka a bounce-back plan

- Give yourself permission to be miserable for a while.

- Baby yourself—by eating ice cream, listening to a wallowing playlist loudly and on repeat, whatever works for you.

- Surround yourself with people who love you. Reach out to family members and friends for support.

- Make a list of things that are making you sad.

- Make a list of things that are still OK!

- Write a letter and don't send it, or write in your journal.

- Stay busy, even when you don't feel like getting off the couch.

- Watch a funny movie and a sad one.

- Exercise, meditate, or go for long walks.

- Do something you've never done before, even if it's as simple as eating at a new restaurant or trying out a new hiking trail.

- Do something nice for someone else, whether it's volunteering or buying a stranger coffee.

- Figure out your next steps.

- Let go and move on.

CHAPTER 7

DON'T GO IT ALONE

I really do not like to organize and plan. Which is ironic, as my husband likes to point out, because that's what I do all day every day in our family. But I do it by default, because on a day-to-day basis, it's my least favorite thing. So when we were starting POPSUGAR, I had zero interest in thinking about formalizing vacation policies, health care plans, promotions, and titles, and organizing the department. I wanted to make POPSUGAR the best place to work, and I had a vague idea of what that would require, but I did not want to suffer through figuring out the specifics. Instead, I found people who not only excelled at that kind of stuff, they enjoyed it. I needed people who understood what we wanted and what we needed and who would work out the details.

We all need help in life, and there is no shame asking for it, whether it's finding the right friends at work or hiring people to make up for your weaknesses. You need people who you can ask for small favors and return those favors when the time is right. Finding your professional support system is a major part of finding a job you love.

STAFFING UP

When I started POPSUGAR, I didn't even tell most of my friends. I worried that they might think it was silly or just not get it, since blogging was a fairly new thing at the time. Part of me wanted to keep the site to myself while I was finding my voice, yet the other half wanted to make sure people saw what I was doing.

So rather than telling my old friends, I found new ones: the strangers who read my posts, and the other men and women who were getting their own sites off the ground. At the time, it was more comforting to find support from the people who understood what I was doing than from my usual support system.

In its infancy, POPSUGAR was one of thousands of celebrity sites around, and new ones were starting each day, so I quickly learned to make friends with other writers who were also one-woman and one-man shows. We had so much news to cover that we would divide and conquer, then cross it all off our lists by linking to one another's stories. That daily link roundup, which I called Link Love, was essential to POPSUGAR's early success.

It felt as though these fellow bloggers were my coworkers, even though I had never met any of them personally and we were spread out across the country. We gave one another advice—about coding, finding images, tools, and navigating legalities—and became friends in the process. We were fond of one another and knew how much hard work we all were putting into our sites. Things even got personal and they congratulated me when Katie was born. Making those friends was incredibly valuable. Rather than see one another as rivals, we figured out how to collaborate. As a result, all of us grew our sites' traffic much faster than we would have alone.

Whatever the endeavor, treating like-minded people as collaborators, not competitors, can make you more successful. I believe that behind every successful person is a strong support system: family, partners, coworkers, mentors, peers, and friends online or IRL. Why go it alone when you can make the right friends? Usually, when we talk about "making friends," we're referring to our social lives; it's incredibly important to surround yourself with people who inspire your passions. But it's equally crucial to make the right friends professionally, whether that's building your personal network, hiring the right people, or finding like-minded companies to partner with.

As a serial tech entrepreneur, my husband had great ideas on how to take POPSUGAR to the next level. Not only did Brian teach me basic HTML coding, but he also understood that I wanted this site to be bigger than me. The site was never named LisaSugar for a reason. ;) Brian knew how to write a fabulous business plan, so we brainstormed how to expand our vision: a modern newsstand that would include all your favorite content in various categories like entertainment, fashion, fitness, food and more, but all in one place. While I was furiously producing content, Brian wrote the outline for our expansion.

I wanted POPSUGAR to be a friendly, safe place but also to be considered the real deal. Over the years, my favorite magazines ranged from *Sassy* to *Entertainment Weekly* and *People* to *Vanity Fair* and *Harper's Bazaar*. I grew up watching *Entertainment Tonight* every night. I wanted to make sure I wrote credible stories that those established brands would be proud to publish. I originally envisioned POPSUGAR as *People*'s fun younger sister: We had high standards about what we would publish and wanted to create relationships with talent, but we also wanted to run those everyday photos of celebrities that make readers realize they aren't all that different from us.

As POPSUGAR grew rapidly, I expanded my daily Link Love to include a lot of these established sites, including *People*, and got on their radar as a result. By 2007, even though we were still a start-up, we were able to create official partnerships with the veteran publishing houses the same way we did with our blogger friends. The more we swapped traffic, the better it was for all of us, even though at the end of the day, we were all competing for the same eyeballs. It's a model we still use today, though now the partnerships have mostly shifted to social media.

Early on, I figured out that my audience loved my site and my point of view, but they would read the same story in multiple places from other voices as well. They were craving information and wanted to see every photo they could. Recognizing that desire was there made me want to write more, as did POPSUGAR's traffic, which was growing at a rate that shocked Brian, who had been working in this space for years and had never seen growth like this, especially with an unheard-of brand. But I could barely create enough content for one site, much less nine more. That's when I knew I needed more people to help me write, ASAP.

THE TWO-WAY JOB INTERVIEW

One thing I love about POPSUGAR is that I am constantly surrounded by smart people who are passionate about what they do. I continue to improve myself by finding people who inspire me and who don't bring me down. Of course, that means I have to hire the right people, and over the years, I've learned a lot about how to identify talent and what to look for in an employee.

Aside from a solid résumé, I want employees who are excited, passionate, and curious about what we cover. They don't have to be clones of me; in fact, that would be boring. They don't have to be just like each other, either. The process differs slightly depending on the position and the department: For an entry-level editorial job, it's about finding smart, passionate people with a strong work ethic. Sure, a candidate who has had four online media internships is great, but that doesn't mean I will dismiss someone who has worked in retail for the past year (you know how I feel about folding jeans!). We need all types of people working toward the same common goal: producing content that will get our readers just as excited as we are. What I'm really looking for is life experience combined with the necessary talent. If it's someone more senior, I'll also look for the ability to motivate and inspire a team. I want someone who is incredibly organized, who fits our corporate culture, and who has a proven ability to get results.

I've always asked the same questions when I interview candidates. I want to know what sites they read online, the TV shows they like to watch, the last book they've read, or brands they love. I want to know what they do in their spare time, because the best jobs are things you would do when you have nothing else to do! I want to hear that they can be passionate about something and hear them explain why. I want to feel their excitement about their areas of interest, whether it's celebrities, healthy living, parenting, shopping, or grammar and writing style. I want to make them comfortable and at ease so I can really get to know them and get a sense of their personality. I need to know if they are going to be a good fit and if we will inspire each other. I also need to sense a strong work ethic. Though our editorial staff is bigger than it once was, we like to stay lean, and there is no room for anyone to slack off.

When you're the one being interviewed—especially at a company that's been on your wish list—don't focus only on trying to get the job. Use the opportunity when you're in the office and meeting with the team to think about whether this is a place you'd be happy working. Do these seem like the kind of people you want to work with? Are they dressed the way you imagine dressing for work? Do they smile less than you would like? Does the office have a funny smell or bad lighting that might get to you over time? If you are getting bad vibes, trust your gut, because you need to feel at home in this space. Yes, you want to make a good impression, but you also need to make sure that this is a place you can grow and be happy. If it doesn't seem like that place, then take note of what feels wrong about it.

WORKING WITH FRIENDS

When we started POPSUGAR, Brian and I immediately hired some of our longtime friends, which was both comforting and terrifying. We have a lot of old friends who we trust deeply, so hiring them and building a business together was a no-brainer. Brian has always brought along past employees to his next gig, and he immediately hired two engineers from past companies who would help us build POPSUGAR. Krista (who is also married to my oldest family friend who I grew up with in Maryland and whose sister Rebecca was our PR turned Mom Director!) left her lucrative job in banking to come do a little bit of everything: model out business plans, run HR and recruiting, and basically anything operational.

I recruited my college best friend, Jamie Saxon Roy, to cover advice for our second website, DearSugar. I was thrilled to have a close friend who believed in what we were doing—even though when she started in February 2006, she was working for free (a realllly good friend!). Brian's sister, Jenny Sugar, was also one of our early employees, and she writes incredible fitness content—in fact, her stories are some of our network's most popular. Another dear friend is our CFO, Sean Macnew. He didn't join POPSUGAR until July 2008, and his wife was on our payroll first. Her name is also Lisa, she is also from Maryland, and she was one of the first people I met in SF when I knew no one! Over the years, we met her boyfriend, then went to their wedding, and now her husband is our CFO. I could not be more proud to have someone so smart running our financials who can also enjoy hanging out at the pool with all our kids.

With our first eight hires, we were giddy with excitement, and the ideas were endless; every day it was like playing company. When you find hardworking people you can trust and that you also like to hang with for an unlimited number of hours a day, you want to keep them close. You also really, really don't want to let them down. That doesn't mean we hire only our friends or that there is always a place for a friend if they come asking for a job. Sometimes, their skills and personalities just aren't the right fit.

Hiring friends has worked for us the same way working together has worked so well for us as a couple. When we hire friends, it makes working late and going out at night that much more fun because we are always brainstorming. Even when we are working, it feels like a good time. We know how to shut off work talk when we need to, and we know when to put other people in charge of managing so there isn't any awkwardness. As we grow as a company, we are still very passionate about what we do, and we can't be rainbows and unicorns all the time. Walk by one of our exec meetings, and you might hear voices being raised, but what might sound like fighting is really just a heated debate over something we are passionate about. Sometimes it's fighting for an investment or head count or an event or other resources; other times it's positioning our story and audience. In the end, we all want the same result: a happy, successful, profitable company. And even if it gets a little ugly at times, we can still have drinks or go to a Giants game and everything is fine again.

When it was time to grow past the comfort zone of our first eight hires, referrals were the next best thing to friends. We were fortunate to find a lot of talent that way, including Nancy (who I mentioned earlier) and Susi May, who launched our Fitness site and now touches everything health- and wellness-related on our sites, including editorial, video, events, and more. Our ninth employee, Kim Timlick, was the first hire we didn't already know, but we shared a mutual friend. Kim was new to writing, but she and I loved the same celebrities, and she read all the weeklies, like me. I could tell she worked hard, based on her previous experience, and she was up for a risk, joining a company that at the time had no funding but that she believed in. Ten years later, Kim is still with us and has had 101 different jobs since her first day. It's just as exciting for me to watch her take on new roles and grow as it was when we wrote our first POPSUGAR stories together. Just like my relationships with Nancy, Susi, Lizzy, and so many others, it's led to a long-term work relationship and friendship that continues to inspire me every day.

At the same time, the new hires were still strangers, and my main concern was whether they could be as obsessed about this business as we all were, or would it just be a job for them? Thankfully, everyone at this point was taking a risk by coming to work for us, so the obsession was contagious, and all three of them are still with us. In fact, a lot of that first "class" of 2006 is still around, which makes me really proud. Without them, I would not have been able to have three kids, grow the company to five hundred employees, and remain happy and healthy.

One of my favorite things about hiring a team is watching them grow. Just as our ten-year veterans say, "Wow, Katie is almost ten?" I feel I have watched them grow up. It's like none of us can believe we are all still here, but we are and we love it. I can still see our editorial director, Becky Kirsch, frozen in time as the twenty-three-year-old who moved across the country for a job uploading photos of celebrities. I will never forget interviewing Angelica Marden, who was employee twenty-eight, at a café on Fillmore Street. I immediately knew she was perfect for us, though not for the job I was interviewing her for, so a month later, I asked her to come back and consider another spot. Today, she is our VP of editorial operations, and I still have a copy of her printed résumé. I initially admired these new hires as smart, ready-for-anything young women, and they still are.

I have also made some of my closest friends thanks to this company, and sometimes you get lucky enough to hire a stranger who becomes a best friend. I was fortunate enough to have Molly Goodson as a partner by my side for more than seven years. She started in January 2007 as employee thirty-three, and she was the first person who I felt could finish my sentences and write exactly what I was thinking, except with more humor, which I loved. She became my partner in all things celebrity and entertainment, traveling and hiring teams in NYC and LA, and launching new businesses and working the Oscar red carpets together. We spent every night online chatting about whatever show we were watching or images we had to post. She and her husband quickly became a part of our family, and even though she left to start her own company, we still have dinner and movie dates almost every week.

THE MUST-HAVE WORK RELATIONSHIPS

Whatever the industry, we meet a handful of people during our careers who can help in different ways. Some are there for emotional support, while others can help us get ahead in networking, but they are all incredibly valuable when building your work-related support system. Here are the types of people you're likely to encounter and what you can offer each other.

- **YOUR BOSS.** The most obvious and usually the most important person to impress, your boss can be an ally, a mentor, someone who challenges you to get better, or someone who makes your life hell. If it's the latter, just be careful who you complain to, because you never know who that boss might be friends with. Going to HR or another higher-up you trust is your safest bet. If you have a boss you love and you find out you are getting a new manager, don't panic. The more managers you have at a company, the more mentors you can turn to for advice, even after they've technically stopped being your manager.

- **THE HR REPRESENTATIVE.** One of the first people you'll meet at a new job, he or she might offer you the job, train you, or just go over the employee benefits with you. Whatever resources HR offers, use them to get the most from your company's offerings: health insurance, 401(k), maternity leave, and vacation policies. HR should also be the first place you go to discuss sensitive topics or personnel concerns you don't feel comfortable discussing with anyone else. Trust them. They are your first ally and have seen a lot of good and bad shit, so they are ready for anything!

- **YOUR OFFICE BFF OR WORK CREW.** Having a good friend at the office, even one whose friendship goes beyond work, is an invaluable part of loving your job. Hopefully, you make many along the way. These folks should preferably be a peer in your department or someone who works in another department. An office BFF understands what you do, can help you solve problems, and shares your sense of humor. They are great to fetch lunch with, happy hour, movies, and more, but try not to use her only to vent, and if you do need to get things off your chest, don't do it at the office. Take a lunch off-site or plan to get a drink and focus on finding a good solution to what's bothering you, rather than just bitching, which can make you both unhappier.

- **ASSIGNED LUNCH BUDDY.** When you start a new job, you might be assigned a buddy or "friend-tor." Often it's someone in a different department you get to know over lunch, or it might be a colleague who is hired around the same time as you. While you might not love the idea of having lunch with a stranger, consider it good practice for future networking. Also, having a support system that stretches beyond your team or even your department can be incredibly helpful in navigating office culture or solving problems down the line.

- **THE COWORKER YOU'RE NOT SO INTO.** Unfortunately, we can't necessarily control who we share an office with. If you have a coworker who drives you crazy, it's up to you to deal with it. If it's someone you don't have to interact with, do your best to avoid her. If it's a peer you think is getting more credit than he deserves, focus on doing the best job you can and prove that you deserve accolades, too. If someone is bullying you or sabotaging you, talk to HR, but otherwise, getting too caught up in your dislike of someone else will just make you disgruntled. Stay focused on the end goal, which is your own happiness and success.

- **YOUR FIRST MENTOR.** This might be your first boss, or it might be another higher-up in your department who understands you and supports you. Other people find mentors in family friends, former professors, or older, wiser women who don't even work in their industry. Whoever she may be, a mentor can be a valuable (and safe) resource for advice, especially when it comes to navigating raises and promotions or figuring out your career path. Think of mentors as your personal advisors. You appreciate their time and guidance. It's great to have multiple mentors throughout your career, and also as a mom.

- **YOUR NETWORKING BUDDY.** This is the friend you often run into at events and find that you connect with. It might be a colleague at your company or someone who does a similar job at another company. Attending events when you don't know anyone intimidates even the most social of butterflies, so it helps to have someone by your side. Even if she is a peer at a competing company, don't view her as competition, because she's incredibly valuable as a collaborator and a sounding board. Whatever issues you are facing—whether it's how to reorganize your team or how to incentivize employees—she can help you problem solve, since she has a similar job and deals with many of the same issues. A peer at another company can be a great secret weapon.

- **YOUR WORK HUSBAND/WORK WIFE.** This person is similar to your work BFF and can be of either gender, but your relationship is deeper and more complicated. Like a married couple, you operate as a team, you can be brutally honest with each other, and you have an intuitive understanding of each other. Your work spouse is probably the first person you go to with good news, and you'll eventually be able to finish each other's sentences. He or she is also a great person to talk to if you need to have a difficult conversation with your manager or a direct report and want to figure out the best way to say it. In my case, my "work husband" is my actual husband, but I joke that Brian has another wife, Melissa, who is his work wife on the other side of the business.

Fun Project Time

If you were starting your own company, who would you draft for your team? Think of it as your ultimate advisory board. It can be anyone from your mom to your friends to Oprah to Jason Bourne (OK, maybe not Jason, since he's already on mine), but think big and get creative. Oh, and make sure they possess these three qualities: Someone you're comfortable enough to cry in front of, someone you want to pull an all-nighter with, and someone who challenges or supports you.

- The big-idea person
- Your work wife/husband
- Your vent (or vice) buddy
- The planner/organizer
- The ultimate advocate/PR/salesperson
- The contrarian
- The networker/extrovert
- The people person
- The problem solver

CHAPTER 8

YOUR PERSONAL ALL-STAR TEAM

I still strongly believe that you need a life outside work. As much as I talk about my work and life blending so much, many of my closest friends have nothing to do with POPSUGAR, and when I am with my family (love you, Mom and Dad!) I tend rarely ever to talk about work. They want to hear about our growth, specific projects, and a night out at the Oscars, but that's when I want to turn it off and enjoy some downtime.

So remember: The relationships you forge outside the office are just as important. Whether it's friends, family, or romantic partners, the people you surround yourself with are part of your team, for better or worse.

FINDING MY LOBSTER

Whether you're swiping right or getting lucky at a bar, you never know when you are going to meet your life partner. Meeting my husband my first week of college was never my plan. It just happened, and I could not be more grateful. I love that Brian knew me when I was young, that he understands the way I have evolved and the ways in which I have stayed the same. Somehow, he maintains that frozen image of me as a seventeen-year-old in his head, even as we grow up and support each other in new and different ways.

I also have a loving Jewish mother. You know what that means, right? I suppose I was lucky that I found my husband young. My mother and all her friends worried incessantly for any woman who was still single at thirty, because that meant she was in some sort of trouble. Which my friends and I all know isn't true. Despite meeting Brian at seventeen, I believe that good things come to those who wait. It's important not to settle but to be picky in this major life decision. You should want to live with your best friend and to love building a life together.

I'm not saying that everyone has to find a life partner. Maybe you have several partners over the course of your life. Maybe you've given up on love and just want friends. Whatever your preference, you need to have key people on your side who are always there for you. The person you choose to share your life with should contribute to your success and happiness rather than interfere with it.

That might mean finding someone in the same industry, or even the same company. Throughout my career, I've worked in offices where coworkers were also dating. Some people think that's the worst thing you can do, but obviously I disagree. I'm all for loving the one you're with, wherever that might be.

But there's also something to be said for finding a partner whose career is completely different from yours. He or she may not know exactly what you do all day, but it can still be incredibly helpful to have someone who can offer advice or reality checks from an entirely different perspective. Don't worry too much about whether this person has enough in common with you or fits your "on paper" image of an ideal mate. No one is perfect, and no relationship is perfect. As Jack Nicholson's character Melvin Udall says in *As Good as It Gets*, one of the best compliments you can pay a woman is "You make me want to be a better man." In any relationship, both people should complement the other in ways that make each of you better than you would be alone.

In our teens and twenties, we often judge potential relationships based on what we have in common, but it's very surface-level: our style of dress, what music we listen to, the books and movies we love, our favorite sports teams, our hobbies. While having shared interests can make a relationship richer, it's not required. I do think couples should find a few activities they can enjoy in their downtime, especially when we spend so much of our lives working, but it's impossible to expect that your romantic partner can fulfill every need you have. That's what friends are great for. If you love going to concerts and your spouse hates it, just find another concert buddy. If you hate seafood, your partner can plan sushi nights without you. All those little things are pretty easy to deal with. That said, it does help to find someone who likes to vacation the same way you do, but even that difference of opinion can be solved with some compromise.

The shared commonalities that really matter in a relationship go much deeper: Do you share the same values? Do you want the same things out of life? Do you have similar visions of what an ideal relationship looks like? Do you want a similar balance between couple time and alone time? These are the far more important questions to ask before settling down.

Me, I wanted someone who was generous, smart, and confident yet still humble. But other than that, it's hard to know what qualities you will value in a person. Brian, for instance, has always been an amazing motivator. Again and again, he made me feel comfortable in anything new I tried. He inspires our family to live as spontaneously as we can. We are also complete opposites in many ways that just work. In an emergency situation, Brian is calm, cool, and collected while I am a nervous wreck. He has an energy about him that everyone loves; it's infectious. And because he is an extreme extrovert, he loves people, and we host parties constantly, which makes my life richer.

As much as I define us as opposites, at the core, Brian and I have a lot in common. We are both East Coast Jews who have an opposite-sex sibling, grew up loving soccer, and enjoy sharing experiences: everything from a great dinner to movie night to a music festival. Before he met me, Brian never really traveled; his first big trip was with my family to Hawaii. He now loves seeing the world and has been to more places than I have, even though he started later in life. From him, I learned to be more spontaneous. He pushes me more than I would push myself in life, but he also keeps me calm. When I was in labor with all three of our children, he was the best coach anyone could ask for.

Brian and I are a rare breed these days: Both of our parents are still married, and so were our grandparents. We dream of maintaining the same loving, beautiful, long-standing partnerships that we've experienced growing up. It's in our blood and we believe in it wholeheartedly. We want our marriage to stand the test of time. We want constant companionship, someone to grow old with who will support us. Most important, we want to raise our girls to-gether with strong values, sweet hearts, and smart minds.

When Brian and I were just starting out in our careers, I never imagined we would work together. It just sort of hap-pened, and it works for us. In the beginning, it was a spon-taneous thing. Everything was moving so fast, and we had so many ideas and adventures. For the first year or so, we even sat at adjoining desks, but as the company continued to grow and our roles evolved, we eventually shifted to sepa-rate desks, then separate floors; but we still walk into the office together almost every day, and who knows when one morning we will decide to sit together again, because we move seats often. We trust each other professionally to make the best decisions and guide our respective teams, es-pecially now that we are fortunate to have a profitable, growing company. Brian knows I trust him to make deci-sions about the business and technology side, while he trusts me with our content and how we adjust our goals each year, week, day, minute. There's only one thing we really argue about, and that is what's for dinner.

OK, we've had our fair share of disagreements at work, too. But we don't lose our cool—at least, no more than any other two executives leading a company. We talk (sometimes yell) it out and provide data and solutions to fight for what we believe in. In the end, I think we work out our conflicts pretty quickly because, deep down, we want the same end result: a successful company that we can get behind.

So to the people who ask, how do you do it? I will say there are both benefits and downsides. The most obvious benefit is that you get to spend even more time with your best friend, the person you decided you want to grow old with. I love being able to leave the house together each morning and not separate until we get to our desks. You also get to share more experiences: You cheer each other on and see more of your partner's accomplishments firsthand. I can see Brian speak at a board meeting or on a panel in front of a thousand people and feel proud of him—something I wouldn't get to experience if we didn't work together.

The downside, I think, is that our three daughters don't get to experience what I saw as a kid: my father walking through the door and being greeted with open arms and huge hugs from my mom. I often say to Brian that we have to make more of an effort to be more loving in our home. We can't take for granted that we are together SO much that our kids won't see our appreciation for each other. When my dad got home, my mom usually also had a glass of wine poured and the table set. We try to bring some of those great evening traditions into our home now. We do family dinner as often as possible, but because Brian and I often come home together, we don't share that same PDA moment my parents had in our home as kids. We have to re-create the warm fuzzy feeling for our girls in other ways. When we are at home with our kids, we don't talk often about work, unless we are sharing a story—it's our dinner routine to go around the table and have everyone share their favorite part of their day.

THE DATING GAME

The relationships in your life that you'll probably make the toughest decisions about are the romantic ones. But having a partner who is on your team, who supports you and complements you, can be an unexpected factor in your success.

Not surprisingly, going on a date can be eerily similar to a job interview: You're a little nervous, you're asking questions and answering them, and you're trying to get a feel for whether the two of you will be a good fit. You and your date might be "interviewing" multiple people at the same time. Sometimes, you send a thank-you note (OK, a text) when it goes particularly well. Other times, you walk away wondering why you haven't heard back when you thought it went so well.

LOVE LOCKDOWN

Of course, part of dating, even if it goes well, is breaking up. It's impossible to talk about breakups without thinking of Lloyd Dobler. John Cusack's character in *Say Anything* (another favorite of mine) pretty much sums up how all of us feel when we have our hearts broken. Disbelief: "She's gone. She gave me a pen. I gave her my heart, she gave me a pen." False hope: "Knowing that just for a minute she felt that and wrote 'I can't help loving you.' That has to be a good thing." Desperation, as he holds that boom box over his head, forcing Diane Court to listen to the song they first made love to. Who among us hasn't wanted to pull the same stunt, forcing the person who broke our heart to feel as shitty as we do?

The truth is, if someone wants to break up with you, there's nothing you can do about it. Not even hold a boom box—or a really high-end portable iPhone speaker—over your head. It's completely out of your control, and it sucks.

Because I met my husband my freshman year of college, I admittedly haven't had as many breakups as some people. But I have helped plenty of friends through them, and the truth is, getting over a breakup is the same as moving past any obstacle, like ending a friendship or leaving a job. You should give yourself permission to be miserable for a while. Listen to depressing music and eat ice cream. Then start the process of getting over it. Make a list of the things you will miss about your ex—and a list of things you won't miss at all. Write an angry letter to the person who dumped you, then don't send it. Make a list of everything you want to be different in your next relationship.

The good news is, when a relationship ends, you have yourself to fall back on. You have passion and ambition and intelligence that is yours and yours only. So reach out to your family members—or those old friends who are like family—and remember who you are and who you were before you even started dating that person. It also helps to spend some time with someone who is outside your circle of friends and doesn't even know "the relationship" part of you.

Once you're past the moping stage, force yourself to stay busy, even if you don't quite feel like it. You may find that you have a shorter attention span, so reading a good book isn't as easy as it usually is. Instead, indulge in a funny movie and take up the whole couch while watching it, like you never could when you were in a relationship. Or watch a tragic documentary to keep things in perspective and remember that it could always be worse. Work out intensely, learn to meditate, or go for long walks. Do something you've never done before, even if it's as simple as eating at a new restaurant or trying out a new hiking trail. Go to a movie alone: Even if it feels taboo, there's absolutely nothing wrong with it, and you might even realize you enjoy it. Buy a new wardrobe item that makes you feel super hot or try something new with your beauty routine. Do something nice for someone else, whether it's volunteering or buying coffee for a stranger.

THE HOME TEAM

When I wake up every day and go to bed every night, I realize how lucky I am to have a partner like Brian. He is the ultimate team player, captain, and referee. He keeps me calm when I would otherwise be freaking out. He is my MVP in my life. Because we hope to have the long, healthy, loving life together that our parents and grandparents have shown us is possible, we work hard every day at making each other happy. From playing FIFA soccer video games in college to teaching our children how to play video games and actual soccer in our thirties and forties, it feels like we've been on one long, thrilling adventure.

I can't help but bring up soccer again, since it's how I spent a large portion of my youth. Playing competitive sports taught me that you simply cannot do it on your own, so you may as well embrace being a team player. At work or in sports, you won't always love all of your teammates, but you still have to be there for them. You can't let them down by skipping practice or slacking off. If it gets to the point where you're not having fun, you can say "fuck it" and find another team.

OK, maybe you can't say "fuck it" when it comes to family, since we can't really choose who we're related to. But we can learn from them, and our families shape who we are. Most of us go through childhood bickering with our siblings, only to grow up and realize they are some of our best friends. It wasn't until later in my college years that I forged a real friendship with my brother, and looking back, I realize how much having him around made me into who I am. Although I love my girlfriends tremendously, having an older brother and being a tomboy made me more interested in playing video games and watching sci-fi than a lot of the activities my girlfriends were doing.

As I got older, the more I realized my extended family had plenty of crazy to go around, and we don't all share the same opinions and values. But having relatives who are nothing like me helped me learn to communicate with and find value in different types of people. If a relationship is completely toxic, you can decide to end it, even when you are related. But otherwise, consider those differences practice for the real world.

Now, friends and romantic partners—those we can choose. Treat that process like building your own personal all-star team. The friends you have growing up don't have to be your friends forever. You can also have friends you stay in touch with even as your friendship evolves, like me and Lisa, my oldest friend from childhood. We were born ten days apart and were nearly inseparable during grade school years, but as we grew up and our interests changed, so did our relationship.

She is artsy and I am sporty, we never went to the same

schools, and we haven't lived in the same city for years. But we still talk all the time and are always there to give each other advice or cheer each other on.

I've always been great at keeping in touch, after years of summer camp and moving to San Francisco away from friends. My husband, on the other hand, is one of the worst at staying in touch, but that's also one of the best things about him. He could be out of touch with a friend for years, but once they get together again, it's like no time has passed. I know it's one of the qualities that people love and hate about Brian, but I love it. He helped me realize that with your best of friends, you can always pick up where you left off.

One of the best surprises of adulthood is that you can make lifelong friends later in life! Yes, it's true. Although it becomes harder to make friends after college, it's totally possible and super exciting when you find those people who you know you want in your life. It can be hard to make friends when you move to a new city, but if you give it time, it does happen eventually. When I first moved to San Francisco, I had a hard time making friends. I was young and married and might as well have been an alien wearing a tutu; people always looked at me strangely when they saw my wedding ring. But over time, I managed to meet a lot of really great friends, most of whom I shared something in common with: Other East Coast transplants, women with curly hair and big smiles. And making friends is often a chain reaction: Those women introduced me to more friends who are still in my life even after moving back East. Some of them even helped me find women to hire!

Much like dating or interviewing candidates for jobs, I can tell pretty quickly if someone will be a good fit. Almost immediately, I start looking for shared values, common interests, a sense of humor I can relate to, and a sense of loyalty. It often starts with friends or something else in common, but beyond that, I also want easy conversation and the urge to keep talking after that first meeting. I gravitate toward friends who enjoy having fun but also prioritize their family—friends who understand the need to work around a nap schedule! I also look for people who can stick to a plan but aren't too high-maintenance. I'm immediately turned off if I meet a friend of a friend and we all head to dinner and she's beyond late or rude to servers or on her phone the entire meal. I trust my gut and know this isn't someone I want more of in my life.

THE RELATIONSHIPS THAT MATTER IN LIFE

Much like the people you meet in your career, your support system outside of work is crucial to creating your dream life.

Though everyone is a little different, here are the types of people you might recruit into your personal dream team—and what to look for.

- **YOUR SIBLING.** This is definitely one of the most complicated relationships, and it varies wildly depending on birth order, how many kids are in your family, how far apart you are, etc. But chances are, whatever strife you have growing up will be less important as adults, when you realize how awesome it is to have someone on your team who understands exactly where you came from. (Apologies to only children.)

- **A CLOSE FAMILY MEMBER (A COUSIN OR AN AUNT).** Not quite as complicated as friendships with siblings or parents, but valuable for the same reasons: They know you in and out, and they get you. If you're lucky like me, they can be just as helpful, influential, and awesome as your best friend or a sibling.

- **YOUR OLDEST FRIEND.** Your friends from childhood won't all be your friends forever, but chances are, one or two of them will stand the test of time. Even if you grow apart or live very different lives, that shared history is a powerful thing and worth holding on to; your oldest friend can remind you how you've changed and how you have stayed the same, in ways you might not realize.

- **YOUR NEWEST FRIEND.** This friend is valuable for the opposite reason. They only know you as you are now, after you've evolved, and without all the baggage. They may introduce you to new things you would have never tried before.

- **YOUR ROMANTIC PARTNER.** You don't always have to have one, but if you do, make sure they lift you up and complement you, rather than bring you down.

- **YOUR COLLEGE FRIENDS.** Again, you don't have to stay friends with your college friends forever, but chances are, you'll keep at least some of them. After all, they are often the first friends you really choose, and they knew you during an incredibly important and formative time.

- **YOUR MOM FRIENDS.** If you decide to have children, you will inevitably meet many parents and make new friends on the sidelines at soccer or through school functions. Not only do you share the experience of parenting, but you also belong to a shared community. Trust me, you need a strong, smart, fun group to help you navigate through all the crazy mommy phases.

- **YOUR COMMUNITY FRIENDS.** Even if you don't have kids, you're likely to make friends as a result of whatever you do outside of work: sports leagues, fitness classes, the local coffee shop, or the neighborhood bar. Don't be afraid to find communities and clubs that can help you meet people, and if you see a familiar face over and over who looks like someone you'd be friends with, smile and say hello. You never know!

- **YOUR FAMILY FRIENDS.** Don't overlook those old friends of your parents who are like family—maybe your mom's best friends, or your parents' couple friends growing up. They can offer advice and comfort and teach you that you can create your own "family" and traditions that go beyond blood relatives.

The Relationship Test

Whether you are single or partnered up, knowing the answers to these questions and sticking to them can help point your heart in the right direction.

- What are the qualities of a good relationship?
- What values do you want your partner to share with you?
- In what ways do you want your relationship to resemble your parents' (or not)?
- What qualities do you look for in a partner?
- How do you like to spend your downtime? Which of those experiences do you want to share with a partner?
- How much of your time do you think you should spend with your partner?
- What things do you still need to have that are your own?
- What is one thing about a past relationship you want to make sure you don't have in the next one?

CHAPTER 9

A WORD ON LOOKS

Throughout my life, I have been surrounded by women suffering from eating disorders. Chances are, you have been as well. You might not know it, but they are among you. They can keep their secrets really well, but when it's exposed, it suddenly seems so obvious. When you witness an eating disorder up close, it is heartbreaking. In high school, I was oblivious to the fact that a good friend was sick even though I knew she was seeing a nutritionist and keeping a food journal at fifteen. It wasn't until I got to college that I realized she was doing a smart thing, trying to take care of herself before a life-threatening eating disorder got out of hand. At college, eating disorders of all types were way more in my face. Binging and purging, excessive exercisers, seriously bad drugs to suppress appetites: You name it, it was there.

It's telling, how often this theme comes up in pop culture, somewhat casually, especially in movies focused on teenage girls, like two of my favorites, *Mean Girls* and *Heathers*. Sadly, it's not all that far-fetched the way the Heathers talk bulimia in the bathroom and the way the teenagers in *Mean Girls* obsess over whether butter is a carb.

Genetically, I am naturally petite and have remained active almost my entire life. Somehow during those pivotal adolescent years that sets the stage for many young women, I was lucky enough to avoid the scarier food and body struggles seen at GW. But that doesn't mean I had zero issues with my appearance. I had no boobs until college and was definitely self-conscious about that. Plus, what I lacked in body issues I more than made up for in hair struggles. I could write a whole book about the decades I spent battling and obsessing over my frizzy curly hair.

The fact is, many of us wrestle with our appearance in some way, but we are fortunate enough to live in an extremely diverse world where appreciating beauty of all kinds has become more normal and even celebrated! I'm a firm believer in learning to love what you were given. That said, if getting Botox or new boobs makes you feel better about how you look, then go for it. At my age, I have plenty of friends turning to Botox, and while I am curious about what I would look like with no lines in my forehead, I'm also terrified of needles. Right now, voluntarily asking for injections isn't high on my wish list. Knee surgery and babies were enough! But I don't begrudge my friends who have gotten injections; they look great and feel better (minus some headaches).

Learning to love yourself isn't easy, and sometimes we need a little outside help. I mean, I still get haircuts in New York, even though I haven't lived there for fifteen years, because I trust my stylist so deeply.

We should strive to find the beauty in everyone, especially ourselves. But that appreciation and acceptance takes time. It is no surprise to me that as women age, we often feel better about the way we look in our thirties than we did in our twenties. I know so many women who look at photos of themselves in their twenties and think, "I would kill for that body now! Why wasn't I ever happy with it when I was younger?" I can't completely explain it, but age, wisdom, and life experience bring confidence and understanding. You realize that it's easier to accept yourself as you are than to constantly agonize over what you would change. I think we start to realize life is too short for all that self-imposed agony.

I know lots of women who struggle with their weight in their twenties but are fitter and healthier than ever in their thirties. Though metabolism can slow with age, understanding your body and working harder to stay in shape makes a huge difference. My sister-in-law, Jenny—who is one of our fitness editors, a yoga teacher, and a vegan—often talks about how it took her five years to lose forty pounds. Not because she started doing yoga or eating vegan (she'd been doing both for years), but because it wasn't until age thirty that she started to figure out the healthy habits that work for her—and that are still working after two kids.

BIKINIS AND CURLY HAIR

My relationship to my body has changed since getting married and having kids. I have plenty of pictures of myself in high school wearing miniskirts, short shorts, and bikinis, but I was usually one of those girls who preferred the one-piece bathing suit. Partly because I was on the swim team and it felt sportier to me, and partly because I liked to be active in the water and I didn't have much to hold up my swimsuit. When I started dating Brian, I moved even further away from the bikinis. I was old-fashioned in that way: It seemed appropriate to be more covered up, since I was in a committed relationship.

After having Katie, I was too distracted with starting a company to realize I'd dropped my pregnancy weight without worrying about it. I wasn't even focused on losing weight, just on nursing Katie and working like crazy. But—as I learned the hard way—rebounding from your firstborn is easier, especially at age twenty-nine.

Losing the weight was much harder after I had my second

daughter, Juliet. But once I got back in shape, I decided it was time to start wearing hot bikinis again, even though I was in my mid-thirties and I hadn't worn a bikini since before I got married. Maybe it's because I worked twice as hard to get my body back to a place where I felt great. Also, over the years, I had seen women of all shapes and sizes being comfortable in skimpy clothes, and it always made me happy that they were happy. Admiring this confidence in other women made me realize I shouldn't be overly critical about my own body.

The silly thing is, pretty much every woman I know feels the same way. When we see a woman who looks great and exudes confidence, we feel empowered, not judgy. Yet so many of us walk around worried that other women are judging us, when really, we are all just worried about ourselves. If anything, we are a little bit jealous not of how another woman looks but of how she feels. We think, "I wish I could be that confident."

Which brings me to my obsession with my hair. Curly, frizzy Jewish hair is not always a pretty sight. When I was little, I was teased a lot, and my brother would call me Medusa. He would actually throw stuff into my hair—coins, Lego pieces, etc.—because it would get lost in there and he thought it was funny. I would have to jump up and down to get it to fall out. I usually wore ponytails because I was playing sports, but mostly because it was easier than trying to figure out what to do with my mane.

It took years to learn how to tame my curls. I have used a lot of the same products since I was thirteen, and lord knows what I will do if they ever get discontinued. I always hated getting my hair done because no one knew how to do it. They would straighten it, brush it out big, put curlers in it, or use a curling iron to re-create the curls. Even then, I thought, what is the point of going to all this trouble? It was the worst! I dreaded family photos because I always ended up hating my hair. For my wedding, I took the time to find the right place and actually train the stylist. I brought my own gels and mixtures and we practiced a few times so all would be perfect on my wedding day. And it was!

Ask any woman with curly hair and they'll tell you that finding someone to cut curly hair is a huge challenge. Thankfully, when I moved to NYC, there were a million hairdressers to test out. I tried a place that specialized in curly hair but wasn't super impressed. Then, I met a coworker with long, wavy curls who raved about her guy. I was thrilled to get in to see Rafael. He worked at a super-fancy salon on Madison Avenue called John Sahag, where Jennifer Aniston and Brad Pitt used to go, back in the day.

The haircut was quite an experience. Not only did this man make me feel like a million bucks, but the technique was like nothing I could have imagined. He blow-dried my hair straight, then cut it around the shape of my face. Fifteen years later, I still see Rafael for my once- or twice-a-year haircuts. My friends think it's funny that I've never found a stylist in San Francisco, but I travel enough to our offices on the East Coast that it's easy to work a hair appointment in. It's not like I'm flying to New York just to get my hair cut (though I can't say I'd never do that, because Rafael is the best). It's just one of those priorities in my work/life balance that helps me find my happy.

Learning to love my hair has been a long journey, but now it's such a special part of me that I can't imagine myself without curls. I never straighten my hair. The only time it's ever straight is twice a year when I get a haircut, and Brian says it freaks him out when he sees me after a haircut because it doesn't even look like me.

My six-year-old has my curls, and she gets compliments on her hair all the time. She understands that her hair is special and unique, and I always reinforce how lucky we are to have our curls. While I appreciate pro-curly messages like Dove's "love your curls" campaign, I'm very picky about what I watch with Juliet. I don't want her to get the idea that curls aren't pretty to begin with!

I always looked up to celebrities with curly hair. Sarah Jessica Parker, Keri Russell, and Rebecca Gayheart (the Noxzema girl in the 1990s) were my curly-haired girls. Over time, they all failed me, cutting or straightening their hair and leaving their curls behind. I realize this is partly because our hair can change with our hormones, but at the time I felt betrayed, like they were crossing over to the other side. In reality, I would never be mad at a woman who wants to straighten her curly hair, but I do think that going with your hair's natural texture makes your life easier.

When someone gets a great haircut or starts carrying a new bag I love, I'm generous with compliments, a trait I share with the rest of our positive, encouraging editors. Frankly, that's one thing I love about working at POP-SUGAR. I am also not shy about taking a compliment, responding with a kind thank-you and a smile. I know from experience in giving compliments that when someone protests too much and shies away from saying thank you, it just makes everyone feel awkward. We should all be proud to take a compliment!

Generally, I avoid commenting too much on other people's looks—especially when it comes to weight. Even if someone has lost a lot of weight that they wanted to lose, I would rather say "You look great!" then make a big deal over their new size. I hate to imply that there is some inherent value in looking skinnier, because really it's about being healthy. I also make an effort not to complain about my own body or appearance in front of other people. Not only because it can foster negative vibes, but also because it's just not that interesting. We should really have better things to talk about!

Aside from compliments, which are always welcome, I don't love it when people comment on my looks either. I remember coming home for my high school reunion after years of not having boobs, and people actually thought I'd gotten a boob job. It was really just a side effect of the pill and a good bra that finally made me curvy. I don't know what's more uncomfortable: being asked if you got a boob job or having to explain your birth control and bra choices.

I've also been asked multiple times if I was expecting when I was definitely not pregnant. To me, this is one of those things that you simply never ask. Someone could be, like, eight months pregnant, and I'll still wait for them to say something. Like many of us, I have a little belly that I can easily hide under my shirt. But now that I've had three kids, my stomach is stretched, and some days it's tighter than others. I can eat dinner and look five months pregnant. I'm OK with that, and it's not going to stop me from eating the prime rib or dessert, but please, don't ask me if I'm expecting. It's just rude. I will never forget the people who've asked me that, and while I try not to hold a grudge, it's still engraved in my long-term memory. :(

Since having daughters, I'm even more sensitive about not making too big a deal about looks. No need to fill their heads with silly appearance insecurities at such a young age. I never talk to my kids about dieting, and they know that people come in all shapes and sizes. We reinforce that by surrounding ourselves with friends, family, babysitters, and coworkers who don't fit any one mold. If anything, I talk about fattening them up because they are all tiny, but that's just genetics and two petite parents. I encourage them to eat more, but I also teach them how to eat well, so if or when they do have growth spurts, they will have established healthy habits.

I am especially invested because I am raising three girls, and I want them to be strong and smart and not obsessed with their weight or their looks. But I think almost all women can relate to that desire. I know women who don't have any kids or who have only boys, and they care just as much about "raising" the young women in their lives to grow up with a positive self-image. The headmaster at Katie's school has two sons but said she always wanted a daughter. Now, she says, she has four hundred of them, which I love. She is a perfect role model for my daughters as a strong, smart, and lovable leader.

As my eldest is in fourth grade, she gets to study health and reproduction in science this year. As a parent, I can't believe we are here already, but I'm realizing sooner is better these days as kids are so exposed to everything at a younger age. Talking about puberty and where babies come from is easier for some parents than others and was a fun eye-opening experience for myself. Already these forty-five girls in my daughter's class are all shapes and sizes. Her closest friend is a foot taller than she is! As parents, we need to do our best to provide a healthy environment and a safe place to discuss everything they are about to face. This is the same mentality that comes back to our sites.

I don't want my daughters to see me fixated on getting pretty. They like to watch me put on makeup, and oddly, one of them loves to come with me when I get my eyebrows waxed. But lucky for me, none of them care to experiment yet, even though some of their friends are into lipstick and stuff. I hope to avoid that as long as I can.

The funny thing is that my six-year-old Juliet and nine-year-old Katie both went through a super-girly phase when they were really into princesses. I had no idea where it came from, because it was definitely not from me. But now, Katie is completely over that phase and couldn't care less what she looks like. She's so "whatever" that I can see my own mother come out in me, begging Katie to just look a teeny bit nicer. Juliet, on the other hand, is very particular about what she wears and how she looks. She cares deeply about her appearance. Maybe it's just her age or a phase, or maybe it's her superpower to tame her curly hair by age six. But I look forward to seeing how this changes over time and watching my girls evolve and develop their own style.

FIND YOUR #OOTD EVERY DAY

Surrounding yourself with the right people plays a huge part in building the self-confidence and comfort that comes with age. The older you get, the more candid your conversations become, and it's so reassuring to find people who are going through the same thing you are. You need friends who will tell you the truth and be your cheerleaders in life, and your friends shouldn't all be just like you. It doesn't matter if you might find them online or in person; people you don't know IRL can still have the power to make you feel uberconfident. You need friends who can help you find the perfect dress or tell you when it's not flattering. You need friends who can prep you for a first date, or give you the rundown on what really happens when you get Botox. Your friends should inspire you to take risks and try new things.

Set out to find your personal style, and don't be afraid to experiment. It might take some time to figure out what really makes you feel good. We often dismiss a certain clothing style or hairstyle because we think, "I could never pull that off." But whatever you think you can't pull off, you can find someone online who is rocking it. It's similar to the way we admire other women for having the confidence to wear a bikini. Let those women inspire you to take changes, because the only thing separating you from the woman who rocks over-the-knee boots or a pixie cut is the ability to own it.

"I can't pull that off" is a potentially dangerous mindset. This way of thinking can hold you back. I am a big believer in stepping out of your comfort zone—whether in fitness or career or dating or pastimes. Trying new things is the only way to discover what you are really passionate about. I'm not saying that you have to try every crazy fashion trend or every hair color, but if you really love a certain look, try it! Experiment with different outfits or hairstyles or makeup and decide what's worth your time and money. Dismissing things before you give them a chance is a surefire way to stop evolving.

A huge part of feeling confident is figuring out what makes you feel your very best. Try to embrace what you were given and make the best of it. If there's something about your appearance that you really can't stand, don't be ashamed to change it. At the same time, try not to judge others for the choices that they make. I love my curly hair, and I smile when I see fellow curly tribe members, but I also don't begrudge women who have decided that the straight hair route makes them happier. To each her own, as long as you feel good.

The same way that I felt better about my body in my thirties than I did in my twenties, so many women feel hotter at age thirty-five and forty-five. I mean, just look at Jennifer Aniston, who is aging fabulously and is hotter than she has ever been. It's all about being comfortable with who you are. Even men, who are notoriously so visual, are attracted to the confident woman in the room. Just make eye contact and go from there. It really does work. You can be standing next to the most conventionally sexy or scantily clad woman, but if you are confident and you smile and make eye contact, you can win.

Feeling good about yourself means having a genuine smile on your face. It means you stand up straight and look at ease with yourself, rather than shrink down and hide. Confidence manifests itself in eye contact and good posture, two things that people always notice even if they can't put their finger on why. You will be surprised how much feeling good about yourself makes you look better.

PROMOTING POSITIVE IMAGE

I want to inspire women to feel self-confident and not let body issues hold them back. I'm thankful that society is finally coming around to appreciating women of all shapes and sizes. When I started writing POPSUGAR, I knew right away that I wanted it to be a safe place for women of all sizes. When I talked about celebrities, I avoided stories about weight gain and kept pregnancy speculations to a minimum, because no one needs that shit.

Along with the celebrity rule mentioned earlier, there is also absolutely no body-shaming allowed. We embrace body diversity and diversity in general, and we don't say anything negative about anyone's looks. This philosophy extends to our office culture: No catty mean girls need apply.

Just as I used to feel kinship with curly-haired celebrities, I want our readers to see women on POPSUGAR that they relate to and who look like them. I appreciate the rise of social media and fashion and beauty blogs for many reasons, but one of the best things about these new Internet personalities is that we now have so many people beyond celebrities and models to look up to. On Instagram, personal blogs, and YouTube, we can see confident women of all skin colors, hair types, and body types who embrace what they were given and inspire us to do the same.

The Internet can also be an ugly place. When I set out to create POPSUGAR, I wanted it to have a positive voice because there were hundreds of other people doing the opposite. It is so easy to be anonymous online that people don't think twice about being rude or just plain mean. So in the beginning, I kept a very close eye on our comments. I wanted people to feel safe and to share with and encourage one another.

As our community expanded rapidly, I was lucky to have a devoted group of very active users who believed in my vision. They helped me monitor the comments and send the trolls packing. I was especially sensitive about our Look of the Day feature. Users would upload photos of their outfits, and our fashion editors would highlight one of the looks each day and tell readers where to buy similar pieces to re-create it. Like Instagram and blogs today, it allowed us to highlight women who weren't models or celebrities, just readers who loved style. The feature was hugely popular, and our audience loved being chosen. Of course, I kept an even closer watch on those comments, because I was very protective of the people who were putting themselves out there. Once again, my core readers would step in to help if anything got out of hand.

Now the community and the comments have all shifted to social media, which makes it even harder to moderate. I encourage our editors to engage with readers and answer their questions so they know we are real people. But when someone gets negative, we don't engage. I have to train our new hires never to take comments personally. I remind them that the nastiness isn't about them. It's coming from an unhealthy and unproductive place. To quote *Mean Girls*, "Calling somebody else fat won't make you any skinnier. Calling someone stupid doesn't make you any smarter. All you can do in life is try to solve the problem in front of you." It's easier said than done, but part of putting yourself out there is dealing with negativity. You hope that for every mean comment on a post, there's someone else who related to your story, or was entertained or learned something new. When the attacks get nasty, the best thing to do is not acknowledge them and just move on.

That's why it's incredibly important to me that POPSUGAR is also a safe and supportive place to work. I want our team to be able to leave behind any negativity they encounter online and find solace in the awesome women around them. I've been told that the vibe at POPSUGAR is a refreshing change from the catty, mean-girl culture they've experienced in the past, and I'm proud of that. We are straightforward and honest when we need to be, but we are also generous with compliments and encouragement.

Just as we want our sites to represent all types of women, our staff is a diverse bunch: women and men from different places with different cultures and different lifestyles. We have all-American girls, hipsters and hippies, proud nerds, recovering punk rockers, fashion and beauty junkies, chic urbanites, women with rainbow hair, and Harry Potter fanatics. One thing I love about our team is that I'm constantly surrounded by people who are experts on all sorts of things. We embrace our differences and are curious to learn from one another.

YOUR #OOTD FOR WORK

The older I get, the less I seem to care about how I look and the less interested I am in going through a lot of trouble. I mean, of course, I do care to some extent, and I want to show up looking clean and cute, but I pretty much get ready in thirty minutes every day from showering to getting dressed to putting on makeup. I'm lucky I don't have to blow-dry my hair.

I love the idea of a uniform. I wore a uniform for six years in school, and so do my girls, and it makes it super easy to get them ready for school in the morning. I love that they aren't consumed by deciding what to wear every day. But I'm not just talking about a school uniform—I also love the idea of a uniform for work. Everyone talks about Steve Jobs and his black turtleneck and Mark Zuckerberg and his gray T-shirts and even Michael Kors and Alexander Wang and the many fashion designers who have their specific uniform. Brian has subscribed to the uniform mentality for years, too. It makes getting ready easy and fast, and it's one less decision to make, considering all the other important things we have to do all day. Most days, you will see me in blue jeans and a silk top, cashmere sweater, or T-shirt. I change things up here and there, and occasionally I get girly and wear cute skirts and dresses, but most often I just want to go to an easy, happy place with my everyday attire and not overthink it.

● **FINDING A PIECE YOU LIKE AND BUYING IT IN EVERY COLOR!** When I find the perfect shirt, I go back and get it in multiple colors and probably twice in white and black, because these will become my go-to pieces. Those shirts that I can turn to when I can't think about what to wear, feel like I have nothing in my closet, or I am rushing to get ready. They are my trusted friends who won't let me down, so I always want a clean one ready to throw on. I feel the same way about shoes in multiple colors!

- **FINDING A FAVORITE STORE OR BRAND.** This is key because you will know your size and fit, and each season you can easily pick out key pieces to update your wardrobe. You can also watch items more closely for when stuff goes on sale.

- **HAVING ONE OR TWO INVESTMENT PIECES.** If you work in a more casual place (like POPSUGAR), still invest in a couple of professional dresses/outfits you can wear on those days you have important meetings and need to dress up.

- **PERSONAL STYLIST/SHOPPER.** Don't be afraid to ask or get help. Most stores have FREE personal shoppers who can help you find key pieces or a special dress and stay within budget. Once they get to know you, they will call you when new items are in or get you early access.

- **HAVING A UNIFORM.** Yes, it can seem boring, but it takes the stress out of trying to impress. It's about learning your body type and figuring out what you are comfortable and confident in and wearing that most days of the week. Bottom line: It just makes life easier. You can still personalize your look in other ways like accessories, haircuts, and lipsticks.

- **DITCHING ITEMS YOU DON'T LIKE.** If you hate wearing dresses, don't force yourself! Go for skirts or pants instead. If you can't find a sweater that isn't itchy, then learn to layer and stop searching for the perfect sweater. I am not a fan of tights, so you rarely see me in a skirt or dress in very cold weather.

Just as many women often feel more beautiful in their thirties than in their twenties, settling into a go-to style takes confidence and perspective that comes with age. I can still have fun trying out new trends, but it's much less important to me than it used to be. I want to be able to look my best without spending too much precious time I could be using for something else.

Like exercise or healthy eating, you have to find what works for you and let that dictate how much time and money you spend on it. Some women love the ritual of putting on makeup, or their ideal downtime is getting a manicure. Other people find joy in putting together creative outfits but never go to the trouble of blow-drying their hair. We all choose to spend our money on different things, be it facials or manicures, handbags or shoes, cosmetic dermatology, or intricate tattoos. Nothing you do for the sake of your appearance should feel obligatory, but if you find that one thing that makes you feel great about yourself, then do it.

Questionnaire

- When do you feel your most confident?

- When do you feel your sexiest?

- What does sexy mean to you?

- What does beauty mean to you?

- Name two totally different people whose looks you love. What is the same (and different) about them, and what do you like about them?

- How long did it take to get ready this morning?

- What part of your getting-ready routine do you hate? Can you just give it up?

CHAPTER 10

THE WORK/LIFE BLEND

I'm often asked, "How do you do it all?" But for me (and probably most people), that frequently asked question never has the same answer. Some days, I feel I'm nailing it and ready to conquer something new. Other days, I'm barely holding it together and figuring things out minute-by-minute.

Not to mention, "it all" has so many layers: Raising three girls when Brian and I both work full-time, and on top of that, our full-time jobs involve running a company. Together. That means sometimes going home to the same person you were in a tough meeting with just a few hours before and resolving the conflicts of both a marriage and a job. We have to figure out how to divide responsibilities at the office and at home, planning our lives around kids' schedules and work travel and trying to make sure not everything happens at once. I do my best to build my calendar around our family, but of course, it's impossible for everything to work out perfectly all the time. I've had to miss many of my daughters' events, which caused serious mom guilt, and I make tough decisions on the work side, too. It's an ongoing struggle to prioritize everything without making myself physically ill or regretting missing out on an important moment for my family or for my company. It's my least favorite part of the work/life blend, but one I find worth fighting and planning carefully for!

Our situation is unique, but what isn't unique is the ongoing struggle of how to do it all. The truth is, work/life balance is hard for a million reasons, no matter your age, relationship status, or how many kids or pets you have. All of us work way too many hours in the United States. Compared with most other countries, we look like a nation full of workaholics. We're expected to be available on our phones after work, or we just feel we should always be on.

Sometimes we do it to ourselves, because if we find work we love, we don't want to leave. Especially if you're good at your job and advancing your career. It just gets harder to check out, to stop looking at your phone every second, to let yourself take a real vacation.

The concept of work/life balance doesn't mean separating my work from my life. It's more like a work/life blend, where everything is interwoven. Here's what a somewhat normal day looks like for me:

6:41

Alarm is set, if I am not already up. But I really do love to sleep, so I try to get every last minute in. I spend the next few minutes scanning for any world news I need to know about, reading and answering e-mails if anything is urgent, anything for my kids I need squared away for the day. Depending on how much time I have left, I also check Facebook and Instagram.

6:50

Shower.

7:00

Throw on some clothes. Usually jeans and a silk top, sweater, or T-shirt, depending on my mood.

7:05

Katie is usually up reading in bed, so I give her a kiss and send her downstairs. Then I sneak into Juliet's room. She likes her sleep (like her mommy) so I slowly wake her up with a kiss on the cheek under dim lights. She needs a few stretches, then I help her get dressed and we go downstairs. I make myself some coffee while the girls are getting set up with breakfast. I usually do a rundown of the day with our nanny: car pools, after-school activities, homework, etc.

7:20

I go back upstairs to put on some makeup and shoes and do anything else that I need to do, like start some laundry, make the bed, or tidy up. Usually, Elle is getting up by this point, too, so I can see her and get her out of her crib before I head out.

7:45

On most days, if there's enough time, I make our favorite kale-pineapple-blueberry breakfast smoothie for Brian and me.

7:55

Brian and I walk Katie and Juliet to school—about five blocks and one of my favorite parts of the day. The girls are chatty, and we enjoy the beautiful city and weather!

8:10 to 8:45

Brian and I usually walk to work together. Some days, I force him into a planning session. Other times, we discuss ideas for apps to build or stories to write. I'm usually e-mailing along the way, too, so by the time we get to work, I am ready to dive in. If Brian isn't with me, I call my mom, my friends, or my coworkers on the East Coast.

8:45 to 5:30

Once I'm at work, the days are all different. I might be interviewing candidates, training new employees, brainstorming with the teams, or meeting with potential partners and brands. But what stays the same are back-to-back meetings with pockets of time when I can do research and send feedback. Most days are spent working closely with video, sales, and marketing, and I also curate our POPSUGAR Must Have box, so at least once a week, I meet with our merchandiser Ricki to test and give feedback on products, plan our monthly themes, and discuss what we want to do next. I often travel to LA and NYC—which means more meetings with teams, partners, and talent—or to trade shows, conferences, and panels.

5:30

I like to be home by six for dinner with the kids, and I tend to leave even earlier here and there to take my shift in various carpools.

6:00

Dinner could be home-cooked, picked up, or ordered in. We like to eat as healthy as we can, with a lot of Italian food and dessert if we are all behaved at the table.

7:00

Bath time for the kids.

8:00

I love this time of night. Once all of the girls are in their pj's, the four of us pile into Juliet's bed and read together. Sometimes our dog jumps into the action, too, but Brian isn't allowed (that energy I usually love just riles the kids up). After reading a few stories together, I spend time with each girl one-on-one. I put Elle in her crib first, where she gets a few more stories, then I go back to Juliet and read with her until lights out around eight thirty, then I'm off to tuck Katie in and give her a kiss good night.

9:15

I'm back online answering e-mail, ordering stuff online, and watching TV.

11:00

I am usually in bed around this time, but most days, I have to force myself to put the phone down and completely shut off by midnight.

· · ·

It's not always easy to fit it all in, between work and kids and marriage and staying healthy, and what works for me won't work for everyone. You have to figure out the blend that works for you and when enough is enough. You have to be willing to admit when you need help and not beat yourself up if something slips through the cracks. You have to be able to shift the scales as the circumstances of your life change and reprioritize when it's time.

FAMILY FIRST

For me, family always comes first. My parents taught me that value through their actions, and because I grew up feeling so loved and fortunate, I want my children to feel the same way. Some people choose to put their career on the back burner so they can stay home to raise a family, or one parent works full-time while the other puts in fewer hours. In my case, working actually makes me a better mother. I value my time with my kids at night, on weekends, and on the morning walk to school so much more because it's precious to all of us. While I love my work, and my career is important, my calendar revolves around the kids' schedule, and having a happy home brings me the most satisfaction.

One of the highlights of my day is when Brian and I take the girls to school. Getting ready can be a challenge as we rush to shower, eat, get dressed, and out the door on time, but once we leave the house, there is great energy and we are all excited to talk. It's incredibly fun for us all to go as a family. Any given week, Brian or I fly somewhere, so on days when I have to travel for work, I try my hardest to take a flight that is after that morning walk.

I also don't let myself feel guilty for leaving work at 5:30 P.M. most nights so I can get home to make dinner or spend time with my kids. It's important to me, and everyone knows I don't check out when I leave the office. I'm usually reading and answering e-mails off and on, and I'm back on my computer at nine once everyone is tucked in. I like to work while watching TV, so I love to dual-task at night. Projects that need my full attention at that point might have to wait until the next day. I also tell our editors not to worry if they have to leave during the day for doctor's appointments or haircuts or dress fittings (we've got lots of weddings!). As long as you do your work well and no one is waiting on you, I say, then do what you have to do.

I want to be an active parent: I volunteer often at the girls' school and make time for field trips or class parties where parents bring treats or do a craft. I'm lucky that it's fairly easy to plan my work schedule around this stuff. I know my kids aren't always going to want me around, so I need to double down during this time when they do.

Within our company and with new families I meet through our daughters' school, I am constantly amazed at how many working moms there are. I'm wowed by how many of us are juggling so much, but it makes me feel so much better when we can coordinate carpools, take turns going on field trips, or let one another find time for a workout. There are some seriously impressive parents who seem to be doing it all, but much of our flexibility exists because of technology: We can work anywhere, anytime. This wasn't always the case. I think about when my dad used to come home from work to watch me play soccer on a Tuesday afternoon, sometimes still wearing a suit while he cheered me on in the pouring rain. Afterward, he would have to schlep back downtown to go back to work—there were no laptops and e-mail to let him take the rest of his work home. He would prioritize watching me play over getting home at a decent hour. I will never forget how important it was to me that he could balance working hard with being present for his family, so I want to give my employees—kids or no kids— the flexibility they need. Lucky for us, we don't have to trek back downtown to finish up; we can work from home, then get even more time with our friends and families.

MAKING YOUR OWN MIX

- **DIVIDE RESPONSIBILITIES.** I have a partner who is also an active parent, and over the years, Brian and I have split responsibilities in different ways. When Katie was born, he started cooking and handling the bills. It just sort of happened, which was awesome for me, because I was tired from a newborn and excited about POPSUGAR but couldn't manage much else. Now he handles car and house stuff, while I manage the kid stuff. It serves the same purpose as managing different sides of the business at work.

- **TEAMWORK.** We also have a team! Cary is a tremendous help in our everyday. She helps with errands; gets snacks ready for car pools; and takes Elle to school, swim lessons, and more. I'm also grateful to be able to rely on other parents. I have a great network of friends who I share carpool duty with and who can help if I am traveling, but I'm also glad to do the carpool once a month, because the conversations the girls have in the car are priceless and I don't want to regret missing out on those moments.

- **AUTOMATE IT.** I'm a firm believer in automating anything that saves me the time and effort of running around town. It's a modern-day must-have if you're trying to create that work/life balance. Not surprisingly, we order pretty much everything online. I place a weekly order at AmazonFresh, use Instacart often, and order from Diapers.com at least once a month. I barely ever go clothes shopping at stores anymore thanks to ShopStyle.

- **SHORTCUTS.** Everyone should allow themselves to take shortcuts. There are so many options now! Personal shopping in the form of monthly boxes, Amazon Prime, Uber, laundry apps, and just about every type of food delivery you can imagine. Don't be too hard on yourself if you have to take even more shortcuts when you're having a super-busy week. Maybe you're committed to packing a healthy lunch every day, but if things are crazy one day, give yourself permission to run out and buy something quick instead. Don't feel obligated to keep your happy-hour plans if you simply can't do another thing that week; your friends will appreciate having you at your best anyway. Just like those times when you can't get to the gym, remind yourself that you're in this for the long haul. Don't be afraid to ask for help from friends or your partner or even your parents, and don't feel bad about accepting help when people offer!

- **SAYING NO.** Brian and I have learned to admit when something feels like too much. Like this past year, when I tried coaching soccer for my daughter Juliet. I'm so glad I did it, but this is definitely one time when I realized I'd overextended myself. As a coach, I was too stressed. Taking off from work early every Friday afternoon made the start of the weekend more hectic than I would have liked. I'm better off being the crazy mom cheering on the sideline and bringing great snacks. And that's totally OK. I may try again when our daughter Elle starts playing in three years, because at least now I know what I'm signing up for.

SURROUND YOURSELF WITH SUPPORT

It's easier to prioritize the things that matter to you if you surround yourself with people who share your values. I expect the people I spend time with to understand the importance of family, whether it's the employees we hire or our network of friends. Our closest friends are just as important as our blood relatives; we love spending time with our friends and their kids, hosting dinner parties and taking vacations together. Because our lives are so interwoven with our work, we also want to create a work family we can count on. Brian and I find ourselves hiring people who have strong family relationships or who treat their friends like family, and as a result, they want to build strong relationships within the company. Selfish jerks need not apply.

At POPSUGAR, we want to create an environment that values the work/life balance and does its best to adapt to everyone's specific needs. Nowadays, companies are way more open to all kinds of circumstances and willing to work with individuals to figure out the best schedule and how to adapt to unique needs. It takes trust and hard work, but once you've built that, you earn the right to ask for more. Companies highly value awesome employees and don't want to lose them, and we're willing to work with people to find whatever their ideal balance might be.

We've heard from our employees over the years that volunteering is an essential part of their work/life balance, but it's hard to fit in. So two years ago, we launched #PSGives, which lets everyone take two paid days off a year to volunteer. Teams will often plan outings together, taking a day to work at a local shelter or charity. I love seeing everyone come back to work clearly feeling so rewarded, and it makes a great team-bonding experience, too.

WHEN SHIT'S OUT OF CONTROL

When I was younger, I felt guilty taking a sick day. At my high school, some girls would take "mental health days." I was always like WTF is that?! In college, skipping a class here and there was a normal occurrence for my friends, but I always felt bad if I ever missed a class. Because my family had saved a lot of money to get me there, skipping class felt like I was failing them, even though many of my peers were doing it. It was easy enough to just go to class and avoid the guilt.

In my first couple of jobs, calling in sick made me even more sick, because it felt like I was letting someone down. Even if I had the flu and knew I had no other choice. I'm still stubborn and go into work when I'm not feeling great, but now the guilt comes from exposing other people to my germs. No one should feel crappy for getting sick. It's a sign you need rest, so slow down and recharge before it gets worse.

I've even grown to understand the need for mental health days. Sometimes, you just need to let your body reset and get into a better space, and if you can do it on a day when you aren't leaving anyone hanging or letting your team down, then I'm all for it. You know better than anyone what your body and brain need, so if you feel like you're getting burned out, you should say something. "Doing it all" shouldn't come at the expense of your health. I'd rather people speak up when they are overworked and ask for help than burn the midnight oil working on a big presentation only to get sick when it's time to present it.

Our employees give so much of their time and energy to our company, and Brian and I are understanding when employees need to take time off to tend to themselves or to their families. We've seen it all: missing work for a spouse in need or personal struggles like miscarriages, divorce, or a sick parent. You should be able to take a day off for a bachelorette party or call in sick when your kid needs to go to the doctor. We also know that our employees value their work/life balance just as much as we do, and we encourage people to take paid time off when we know they haven't in a while.

I think it's especially important to treat yourself to real time off, because even the hardest workers can't work hard all the time. Sometimes you just need a vacation, and if you can't tell when it's time for a break, your coworkers probably can. ;) It's essential to have that time away from work to reset, clear your head, and try new things. And as long as you're not totally screwing anyone over, don't feel bad about leaving your team behind for a few days or weeks. Take them up on their offers to help out in your absence, and repay the favor when they take a vacation. Similarly, set a positive example and leave everything in a good place so your coworkers understand the importance of having a solid plan when they're out of the office. Part of being a loyal employee is knowing how and when to take time off, and the longer you work at POPSUGAR, the more paid time off you get every year.

Vacation helps clear your head and get you back to a creative, more energetic place. It could be a week or two, but a day or two here and there can make a huge difference, too. If you can afford to go away and experience a new place and a different culture, then great! But if you can't swing a trip or you don't want to plan one, take the time off anyway. Stay home and rest, explore a new neighborhood, clean your closets, volunteer, or read a book that's been sitting on your nightstand for months. What you do with your time off is up to you. Maybe it's renting a house with friends or traveling with your BFF. Many of my friends insist on weekends away with their spouses and without their kids. Since Brian and I work together, we never really feel that pressure; we'd rather spend vacations with our family. You need to find out what's most important to you.

Vacations are a way to reward yourself for your hard work, and they're especially rewarding when you know you've really earned it. When we first launched POPSUGAR and had a brand-new baby, vacations just weren't a luxury we had time for. But I knew this was only temporary. Growing up, vacations were a special treat for my family, and I wanted my kids to enjoy the same treat.

When Juliet was about six months old, we took a much-needed trip to Maui with our two girls. Traveling with two kids knocked us on our asses at first, but after the initial adjustment, we fell into vacation mode and got some much-needed rest. It was so special to have so much uninterrupted time together with our kids. We were supposed to be gone a week, but at the last minute, Brian spontaneously decided we should stay for five more nights on another island. We were having so much fun, and everything was running just fine back at the office without us. It was a huge turning point in our personal lives to be able to be out of the office for that long and feel OK about it.

GOLD STARS FOR EVERYONE INCLUDING YOURSELF!

Life shouldn't be divided into the work period and the fun period. As much as you can, make every day count. Don't wait until you retire to enjoy the money you worked so hard to earn. It's morbid, but you never know if you'll actually get to enjoy all the fun stuff you're waiting to do.

One thing I love about the younger employees we are hiring now is that they seem less materialistic than some of the generations that came before. In general, the twenty-somethings who work with us and read our sites understand the importance of investing in experiences. They'd rather spend their money on travel and music festivals than on a Birkin bag or expensive jewelry. Finding the perfect job that makes them happy is more important to them than making lots of money. Of course, finding that perfect job can be stressful, which can throw off the work/life balance. That's why it's important for companies like ours to adapt to their needs, place a value on vacation time, and prioritize the health and happiness of our employees.

While I'm very proud of the success I've had, I also understand that monetary and material success isn't the only measure of success. Having money makes a lot of things easier, but it's not the be-all and end-all. Happiness doesn't magically appear when you hit a certain salary.

A truly balanced life requires both happiness and satisfaction, which are two distinctly different rewards. Money and material things can make us happy. So can seeing a great movie, enjoying a bowl of ice cream, or being really excited about your outfit that day. But satisfaction is far more rewarding. Satisfaction comes from overcoming obstacles, solving problems, or doing something that challenges you and achieving it. You need both types of rewards to feel truly content.

Which isn't to say that material goods can't bring you satisfaction, as long as they represent something meaningful. It can be incredibly satisfying to buy yourself something nice with money you earned. It's the difference between getting a check from your parents on your birthday and getting a raise at work because you worked hard and earned a glowing performance review. The first car you buy with your own paycheck will mean a lot more to you than if your parents bought you a car when you were sixteen. Brian loves to tell the story of saving money from his paper route to buy a car, because he's still proud of it. The fact that he earned it makes it a story worth telling.

There's nothing wrong with treating yourself to things

you love as a reward for your hard work. It's satisfying and it keeps you humble. Whether it's a designer handbag or tickets to a music festival or a special meal at a nice restaurant, a thing becomes more meaningful when you buy it with money you earned. You treasure it more; you take better care of it. It makes you more appreciative of everything you have. No matter how successful you become in life, it's important not to become so jaded that you cease to appreciate the material things you're acquiring. And you should never feel guilty for spending money on things that make you feel good or make your life fuller, whether it's a great haircut, a cooking class, a SoulCycle class, or a spa day.

Life is just too short to deny yourself the things that make you happy. As much as I value hard work and staying healthy, I also believe in indulging in what you love, whether it's a favorite food, a bottle of wine, a handbag, or a pedicure. Some people prefer a great cocktail, while I'd take dessert any day. Indulging can mean making time for things that make you happy, like a girls' night out or a date night with your spouse, or spending money on self-improvement by hiring a personal trainer or taking a coding class. Giving yourself permission to indulge means not feeling guilty about all those so-called guilty pleasures. Whether your biggest vice is chocolate or whiskey, pretty much all of us can appreciate taking a great vacation or binge-watching a TV show.

Indulging is important for so many reasons beyond just

pleasure. It's a way to reward yourself for working hard or to make you feel a little better when times get tough. Indulging allows you to check out for a little while and avoid whatever is causing you stress or to break from your routine and do something unexpected, like go on a last-minute trip or to a concert on Tuesday night. Sometimes you have to give yourself a break from following all the rules. So don't worry about how many calories you eat on Thanksgiving. Order dessert when you want it. When you're really craving something, denying yourself will just eat you up inside and make you miserable. Plus, that bliss you feel when you really enjoy something you love can set a standard for what it feels like to feel good. Letting yourself live a little makes you appreciate your life more.

It's important to find little indulgences that are innocent and carefree. Because there is a difference between indulging and overindulging, and it can be tricky at times. When I say "indulge," I don't mean at the risk of your health. I'm not recommending that anyone go down a path that will affect their health or bankrupt them. Some vices are best enjoyed in moderation or not at all, and if it's making you feel worse instead of better, it's time to reevaluate.

The obvious example is drinking so much that you spend the next morning puking. Thankfully, hangovers are a very effective reminder not to overindulge, but if you're doing so much of anything that it's affecting your social life, your job, or your health, you're probably doing too much of it. A little retail therapy is fine, but not if you're racking up lots of credit card debt. There's nothing wrong with an indulgent meal, but that doesn't mean you should be overeating every day to the point that you feel ill. The luxury of indulging requires the responsibility of knowing when it's time to quit or ask for help.

When shit happens, sometimes ice cream or whiskey just calls out to you. It's totally fine if you give into and enjoy every indulgent bite or sip. Indulging can provide a little bit of pleasure during really rough times, and when you've just gone through something awful, you don't deny yourself a treat. Just be cautious if you're indulging as comfort and make sure it's not making things worse. For instance, having cocktails with friends might help you feel better after a breakup, but getting drunk at home alone usually only leads to more sadness.

At least that's what people tell me. That's all I have to go on, because I can count on one hand the number of times I've been drunk. I am not a drinker, and I never have been; I just never really liked the taste of alcohol. I make funny faces every time I try something new, which Brian finds highly entertaining. While I will never understand the value of a realllllllly good wine or an expensive whiskey, I also don't (literally) piss my money into a toilet. I won't judge anyone who prefers to spend their money on booze. I'd just rather spend my hard-earned cash on travel and good schools and a killer handbag that will last years.

Still, we all need something to give us a little boost, so I'm gonna come right out and admit that I've definitely used retail therapy to make me feel better. The one time in particular I remember buying something to soothe a broken heart was when my dog Jack died. For months, I'd been eyeing this one dress: a cute, perfect summery black dress that I spotted on a few celebrities. Every time I saw it, I'd think, "That's so me!" This was a purchase I'd normally balk at, but for some reason, right after Jack passed, I went into the store looking for it. I remember telling myself, just buy it so you don't have to keep thinking about it every day.

Four years later, I still can't believe I basically bought a dress because I was sad about my dog dying. Still, I love that dress. It's beautiful and well made and I wear it often. And every time I do, I think of Jack and I smile. The double pleasure I get when I wear the dress cancels out any buyer's remorse I could possibly feel.

If you'd rather comfort yourself with whiskey instead of dresses and handbags, no one should judge you. As I've looked for ways to take the edge off with three kids, I will enjoy a glass of wine here and there. But most of the time, I hate how it makes me feel, or I wake up and I can't sleep. The next time, I have to ask myself, do you really want this? It isn't easy to let go of a vice, so why should I work hard to form one? Life is too short not to indulge, but make sure you're indulging in something you really love.

How I indulge has changed since I became a mom. As a

parent, I'm more concerned with providing for my family and being a more complete person. Treating myself means treating my family, too. The fact that I love to travel means that my kids get to enjoy the benefits of nice vacations. My dad was the same way: He worked very hard, but when he took a break, he took us on vacation. It thrilled him to be able to provide for his children in a way that his parents couldn't. Making his family happy made him happy.

But my parents didn't give us *everything* we wanted. They were strict when it came to schoolwork, having good manners, and being a team player, so my brother and I did as we were told and ended up being pretty well-behaved kids. They taught us to be independent and entertain ourselves, and we were good about sharing—all things I am trying to emphasize with my own children. I'm trying not to spoil them, but it's hard. At first, Brian and I thought we would be way harsher parents, but when you have kids, everything they do is so cute—even the tantrums, although not at that exact moment. We set up guidelines and reward good behavior and have no problem taking things away when they break the rules.

Because my dad made me get a job every summer, I always knew that whatever we had was the result of hard work. I didn't care about acquiring "stuff"—clothes or purses or fancy makeup—until I could afford it on my own. The great thing about working hard and making your own money is that you can decide how to spend it. You are the keeper of your own work/life balance. When you're successful, you can make time for the things that are important to you—whether it's dating or spending time with your kids or caring for a sick parent—and shift those priorities around as your lifestyle changes.

In the ongoing puzzle of balancing work and life, it's inevitable that some things will fall through the cracks. For Brian and me, it's decorating. We always joke that someday we will hang stuff on the walls and actually decorate our beautiful home. Though we have done some things to make it very livable, our house is sort of just the place where we live. We have a life that other people might envy, but if you came to our house, you might think we had just moved in! We could definitely stand to invest some time and money into window shades and rugs and furniture and even some art. But we don't have the time to commit to that right now, so it's more chaotic than we'd like.

At this point in our lives, we'd rather use our valuable time for family dinners, the jobs that we love, and spending time with our friends and their kids. We also prioritize our date nights, because despite having three kids and running a company together, we also love being a couple. I'm still a night owl but now I have to wake up early, so by the end of every week, I'm totally beat. Going to a super-early dinner (like five thirty) and a seven o'clock movie with Brian on Friday night is my favorite thing to do. It's my night off from putting the kids to bed.

Even with the craziest schedule, we all need to find those little things that make us happy. Balancing your work and life means nothing if you aren't also taking care of yourself and your mental health. Even if it's something as simple as putting a pen to paper: I have this weird obsession with paper. Something about the careful act of writing on paper just makes me feel better, and despite my very digital line of work, I refuse to give up my paper planners.

I try to find other moments of peace during the day when I can calm my brain, like taking long walks and seeing movies. I also believe that every day, we should all genuinely say "thank you" to someone, whether it's remembering to call your mom and tell her you love her (love you, Mom!), giving positive feedback to a coworker, encouraging a friend, or helping a stranger. Doing something nice for someone else will remind you that there is a balance to the universe even when your life feels out of control. Saying "thank you" makes you feel better about yourself and the world. All the exercise and healthy eating in the world can only do so much if you don't also prioritize your happiness.

The Ultimate "Power Your Happy" Bucket List

**A list of the big and little things to check off
as you create your dream career and life**

- Make an epic list of things you love (and add to it every year!).

- Take an online personality test.

- Draft a two-year plan that you're never afraid to update.

- Try something new every three months.

- Get an internship during college.

- Write in a journal every night for a month straight.

- Volunteer once a month.

- Go see a movie alone.

- Take a vacation alone.

- Keep a running list of personal triumphs.

- Make friends with people older than you and younger than you and pay attention to what they're talking about.

- Throw yourself into an unfamiliar social situation (personal or professional) every few months.

- Aim to read a book a month. (If you are an avid reader already, aim for one hundred in a year!)

- Start a healthy habit and do it for ninety days (e.g., a new exercise class twice a week, walking to work, etc.).

- In every job, keep a running list of your accomplishments.

- Attend a networking event and make sure to meet three new people.

- Write a killer résumé and creative cover note.

- Ask for a raise or a promotion.

- Move to a new city, even if it's just temporary, but be open-minded that it could last longer.

- Find at least five healthy foods you love.

- Learn to cook a recipe passed down in your family.

- Save up money to buy something on your wish list.

- Write a job description of the job you want to have (even if it doesn't exist yet!).

- Overcome an obstacle.

- Come up with a few conversation-starting questions you can use in any situation.

- Take a big risk.

- Find a partner who complements you and lifts you up.

- Write a letter you never send.

- Play a sport.

- Find a great hairstylist.

- Identify your signature office style.

- Spend a holiday away from family.

- Learn to speak another language, play an instrument, or code (or another skill that challenges you and requires discipline).

- Discover your perfect work/life blend.

EPILOGUE

ALWAYS EVOLVING

Over the years, as I've tried my best to work hard, play nice, and be a great mom and partner, I also got help and guidance from others. Whether it's my family, friends, co-workers, or favorite SoulCycle instructors, you never know where something will inspire you. The following mantra is one of my favorite things about Ian's class. He was the first instructor I ever had and still one of my favorites. After having our third daughter I knew I needed a new outlet, and as much as I thought I wouldn't like the "soul" part of SoulCycle, it turns out I was wrong. Ending my weekly Saturday morning class (if I don't have a soccer game) with Ian's words truly makes me a happier person:

*May we walk forward with compassion in our hearts
and may we replace jealousy with joy. And at the
end of the day, always remember that all that you
need is vision to see where you are going, strength to
get you there, and faith that you will end up exactly
where you deserve to be.*

—Ian McAndrew, my
SoulCycle instructor

I'm almost two decades older than some of our awe-some editors (which is hard to believe, now that I actually say it), and while it can be sad and silly at times, I love being surrounded by young talent. All my life, I've been that in-the-know friend who keeps up with pop culture and with what everyone's talking about. Many of our editors are also that friend: the one all their friends come to when they want to know about new trends, tech, or beauty products.

None of us wants to stop being in the know, even if we're older than we used to be. We're still obsessed with keeping up with the latest apps, music, and TV shows. Spending all day on the Internet helps, but it's also crucial to keep your mind open. Nothing makes you sound old like closing yourself off from new things and saying, "That makes me feel so old!" If you feel old because the world is changing around you, that's on you. In an industry that's constantly changing, you have to keep adapting.

If I hear my daughters or my younger writers get excited about something, I immediately gravitate toward it, especially if it seems like something I'll absolutely love or that will make my life easier. I always tell my team that we should be in the know but not know-it-alls. We don't think we're any better than our readers for knowing something they don't know yet. Our job is to be genuinely excited about the new things we want to share, and that means constantly finding new things to be fans of.

Being adaptable makes you a better employee, no matter how far along you are in your career. It's also a good skill to hone in case you need to make a major change. You never know when you're going to have a mid-career crisis: Your priorities can shift after having kids or just because you get bored. Krista took a huge risk when she joined POPSUGAR and left the world of finance, where she had worked for years. But watching her take on an entirely new job as our managing editor was inspirational. She wasn't afraid to ask questions and learn from editors with traditional journalism backgrounds, even if they were younger than she was, and I appreciated her ability to teach us all the stuff we didn't know, like management best practices and dealing with expenses. After becoming a mom, her priorities changed, and she wanted a new role. She's now in a completely different job as our head of corporate culture and citizenship, and she's still kicking ass making POPSUGAR one of the most fun companies to work at.

I want POPSUGAR to continue evolving as well, whether it's launching new businesses or shifting our priorities. We always knew we wanted to hire all different kinds of talent, cultures, and backgrounds, and we are very committed to hiring awesome women: Our staff is 75 percent women with an exec team that's split 50-50 male and female. We also have a much higher percentage of female engineers than most companies. As we grow, we are making an even more conscious effort to be balanced and culturally diverse. We want our employees to represent our audience, which is an increasingly global and diverse group.

Running a company, it can be hard to keep up sometimes, but it also staves off boredom. I love that I've managed to remain a perpetual student eighteen years after completing my formal education. Even after you've achieved your version of career success, you have to be willing to admit that you still have a lot to learn, get out of your comfort zone, and expose yourself to new challenges. Learning a new skill isn't just fun, it's also very satisfying. It gives you something to be proud of. That's why it's important to me to keep trying new things and meeting people who can introduce me to new ideas and skills. As long as I keep moving, both physically and figuratively, every day continues to be an adventure.

ACKNOWLEDGMENTS

First I want to thank all my amazing coworkers, those who have helped build POPSUGAR into the powerhouse it is today. Being able to create such a large extended family has been such a joy. And to those of you who helped take on more of my day-to-day so I could find time to write this book, an even bigger THANK-YOU!

To my friends and family who have helped give me the confidence to keep stepping out of my comfort zone and who inspire me to be happier than I ever thought imaginable.

To Nancy Einhart, without whom this book would never have been written so quickly! Thank you for taking so much time to gather ideas from my head, grammar geeking and then organizing everything on the pages so eloquently. It's been such a pleasure working with you and growing up with you for the past ten years. I look forward to many more adventures and knocking things off our bucket list together!

To our rock-star head of marketing at POPSUGAR, Anna Fieler, thank you for your advice, encouragement, and help during this entire process.

To Maggie Ha and Meg Cuna, thank you for making everything look so chic.

To all my friends at Dutton who helped mold our vision into reality—especially my editor, Jill Schwartzman, for guiding me on this journey.

Thank you to the hilarious and wonderful Andy McNicol from WME, who always kept things real and made sure we ended up with something everyone was *happy* with.

To Anissa, Aimee, Cary, and Jill—thank you for loving our daughters and brightening our everyday.

To Sir Michael Moritz and Jonathan Kaplan, for believing in our vision and team. Your advice and guidance have been much appreciated, and your friendship is priceless.

To my parents: You are the best. Your unconditional love support and guidance over the years is much appreciated.

To my children: You are my sunshine. My lifeline. The best thing we ever created. I can't wait to see where you all end up!

To Brian: What more can I say? Thank you for getting me water on my eighteenth birthday. :) There has never been a better life decision than committing my life to you. xoxo, baby

WHAT POWERS MY HAPPY

SPECIAL SECTION EXCLUSIVELY FOR TARGET

8 STEPS
TO A HAPPY DAY

1. Coffee to start! Iced tea and Vitaminwater throughout the day.
2. Eat breakfast. (Number one rule: Don't skip it!)
3. Never leave home without my 11" MacBook and my iPhone.

4. Get outside and go for a walk.
5. Keep my inbox at zero unreads.
6. Call a friend or family member.
7. Eat chocolate.
8. Wind down on the couch, watching TV and drinking warm water with lemon.

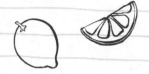

8 EASY WARDROBE OPTIONS
THAT MAKE ME HAPPY

1. A bomber jacket
2. Skinny jeans
3. V-neck T-shirts

4. A-line dresses
5. Silk shirts
6. Sporty sweaters
7. Cutoff jean shorts
8. Sneakers

6 ESSENTIAL
POWER BAGS

1. A classic tote—big enough for a laptop, diapers, and snacks and perfect for travel
2. A trendy clutch for fancy occasions
3. A luxury investment piece

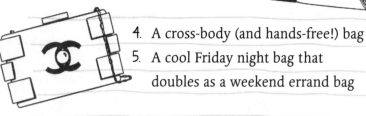

4. A cross-body (and hands-free!) bag
5. A cool Friday night bag that doubles as a weekend errand bag

6. A roomy beach bag that doubles as a carry-on

5 ESSENTIAL
POWER SHOES

1. Chic but comfy sneakers

2. A pair of sexy heels

3. Modern loafers

4. Moto boots

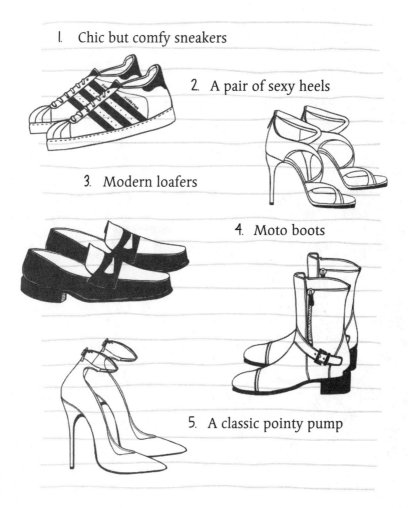

5. A classic pointy pump

MY HAPPY PLACES

- The beach
- SoulCycle
- A bubble bath
- Dance party with my kids
- Movie night

- Ice-cream outing
- Dinner at our neighborhood restaurant
- Park dates
- Swimming

QUOTES THAT MAKE ME HAPPY

- "Nothing is impossible; the word itself says 'I'm possible'!" —Audrey Hepburn

- "Do, or do not. There is no 'try.'" —*Star Wars* (Yoda)

- "It is our choices, Harry, that show what we truly are, far more than our abilities." —*Harry Potter and the Chamber of Secrets* (Dumbledore)

- "The purpose of our lives is to be happy." —Dalai Lama

- "I was just totally clueless." —*Clueless* (Cher Horowitz)

- "Oh, well, my aspiration in life would be . . . to be happy." —Beyoncé, "Pretty Hurts"

MY FAVORITE BOOKS

- *Valley of the Dolls*
- *The Catcher in the Rye*
  (and *Nine Stories* and *Franny and Zooey*)
- *Shoeless Joe*
- *Gone Girl*
- *One Flew Over the Cuckoo's Nest*
- *Shopgirl*

- *A Million Little Pieces*
- The Sweet Valley High series
- The Baby-Sitters Club series
- *Superfudge*
- The Harry Potter series

MY ALL-TIME FAVORITE MOVIES

- *Clueless*
- *Good Will Hunting*
- *Back to the Future*
- *Top Gun*
- *The Secret of My Success*
- *L.A. Story*
- *Reality Bites*
- *Fight Club*
- *Parenthood*
- *Father of the Bride*
- *Beetlejuice*
- *Dazed and Confused*
- *Heathers*
- *12 Monkeys*

- *Star Wars*
- *Romeo + Juliet*
- *Jerry Maguire*
- *The Breakfast Club*
- *Dead Poets Society*
- *Almost Famous*
- The Bourne series
- *The Notebook*
- *Mean Girls*
- *Frozen*

MY FAVORITE TV
SHOWS OF ALL TIME

- Friends
- The X-Files
- The Sopranos
- Breaking Bad
- Sex and the City
- Seinfeld
- Felicity
- The Wonder Years
- Alias
- Gossip Girl
- Lost
- 24
- The O.C.
- Dawson's Creek

XOXO,
gossip girl

F·R·I·E·N·D·S

THE SONGS ON MY ULTIMATE PLAYLIST

- "Stronger," Britney Spears
- "Send Me on My Way," Rusted Root
- "You & Me," Dave Matthews Band
- "Freedom," George Michael
- "Shelter from the Storm," Bob Dylan
- "It's Oh So Quiet," Björk
- "All of the Lights," Kanye West
- "History," One Direction
- "Fix You," Coldplay
- "Only Love," Mumford & Sons
- "Somebody to Love," Queen
- "Escapade," Janet Jackson
- "Tiny Dancer," Elton John
- "Pretty Hurts," Beyoncé
- "Better Man," Pearl Jam
- "I Shall Believe," Sheryl Crow
- "Me and Julio Down by the Schoolyard," Paul Simon
- "All I Want Is You," U2
- "No Rain," Blind Melon

& Generous helpings of Madonna, Michael Jackson, Justin Timberlake, Billy Joel, Eminem, the Beastie Boys, and Bob Marley

THESE ARE A FEW OF
MY FAVORITE THINGS

Candy

Vitaminwater

Iced tea

iPhone

Lemons

Pizza

Sneakers

THESE ARE A FEW OF
MY FAVORITE THINGS

Bags

Sunglasses

Books and TV

Lip balm

Stars and rainbow illustrations

Emojis

& My family, obviously

SECRETS TO PERFECT CURLS

- Don't brush your hair when it's dry. EVER!
- Start with a shower to reset the perfect wet head.
- Shampoo two to three times a week, max.
- Go heavy on conditioner, every time. (Pantene is my signature scent and has been since high school.)
- Brush your hair once the conditioner is in, wait a few minutes, then rinse it out (but not completely).
- Towel-dry your hair.
- Apply mousse to your entire head.
- Apply hair gel all over. I swear by Matrix Vavoom Forming Gel and TIGI Bed Head Control Freak Serum.
- For defined curls, apply the gel section by section. It makes a difference, so I do it for special occasions.
- My secret trick is putting my hair up in a tight bun.
- Keep it in bun for at least an hour (up to three), then release your hair. :)

MY FAVORITE HOLIDAY
"HAPPY EVERYTHING" CARD

MAY THE
**SUGAR
FAMILY**
BE WITH YOU

I like to end the year by
sending loved ones well wishes.

Illustration by Thomas Brush